Words Make a Way Through Fire

"Cyra Dumitru has written with profound heart and soul for so many years, and this is her most crucial, personal work yet. With a voice that always illuminates, then heals, she offers her family's own difficult story with grace and love."

—NAOMI SHIHAB NYE, recipient of 2024 Wallace Stevens Award for Lifetime Achievement, Academy of American Poetry

Words Make a Way Through Fire is a stunning testament to the power of poetry to hold and heal the deepest ruptures of the human heart. Cyra Sweet Dumitru has carved a path of exquisite vulnerability and strength, allowing language to be both salve and compass. Her storytelling and poetry unfurl with raw truth and grace, offering a courageous invitation to witness the unthinkable and, through that witnessing, to emerge more whole."

—SUZANNE ANDERSON, author of *You Make Your Path by Walking* and *The Way of The Mysterial Woman*

"When a gifted writer and poet can transform trauma into a triumphant healing of self and others, we can all celebrate! Thank you, Cyra, for helping us remember that, as in birth, so much good in life can come from suffering. We can emerge from the ashes of despair to a deeper understanding of ourselves."

—ALICIA B. BRIDGELAND, PsyD, Clinical Psychologist

Words Make a Way Through Fire

Healing After My Brother's Suicide

Cyra Sweet Dumitru

SHE WRITES PRESS

Copyright © 2025 Cyra Sweet Dumitru

"Gott spricht zu jedem. . ./God speaks to each of us. . ." from RILKE'S BOOK OF HOURS: LOVE POEMS TO GOD by Rainer Maria Rilke, translated by Anita Barrows and Joanna Macy, translation copyright © 1996 by Anita Barrows and Joanna Macy. Used by permission of Riverhead, an imprint of Penguin Publishing Group, a division of Penguin Random House LLC. All rights reserved.

"A Cloak" (six-line excerpt) By Denise Levertov, from SELECTED POEMS OF DENISE LEVERTOV, ©2002 by The Denise Levertov Literary Trust, Paul A. Lacey and Valerie Trueblood, Co-Trustees. Reprinted by permission of New Directions Publishing Corp.

Excerpt of *Free Play* by Stephen Nachmanovitch
courtesy of Penguin Random House.

All rights reserved. No part of this publication may be reproduced, stored in a retrieval system, or transmitted in any form or by any means, electronic, mechanical, photocopying, recording, or otherwise, except for brief quotations in reviews, educational works, or other uses permitted by copyright law.

Published in 2025 by
She Writes Press, an imprint of The Stable Book Group

32 Court Street, Suite 2109
Brooklyn, NY 11201
https://shewritespress.com

Library of Congress Control Number: 2025909818
ISBN: 978-1-64742-952-2
eISBN: 978-1-64742-953-9

Interior Designer: Katherine Lloyd, The DESK

Printed in the United States

Names and identifying characteristics have been changed to protect the privacy of certain individuals.

No part of this publication may be used to train generative artificial intelligence (AI) models. The publisher and author reserve all rights related to the use of this content in machine learning.

All company and product names mentioned in this book may be trademarks or registered trademarks of their respective owners. They are used for identification purposes only and do not imply endorsement or affiliation.

For David Rockwell Duff Sanborn
Beloved son, beloved brother
October 12, 1954–February 9, 1974

For information on suicide prevention or
to find support when living the aftermath
of a loved one's suicide, contact:

American Federation for Suicide Prevention
afsp.org

If confronting a crisis:

Suicide Crisis Hotline 24/7
Dial 988

or

Text TALK to 741-741 to text with
a trained crisis counselor for free 24/7

Veterans Crisis Line:
Send a text to 838255

Contents

Preface 1

What To Make of Poems That Help Tell This Story 5
   My Brother's Cup

Part One:
My Brother David and the Dreams

1   The Grounding of Water in Early Childhood 11
     Revisiting a Childhood Beach When I Am Fifty

2   That Reverberating Night in February 15

3   Immediate Aftermath 24
     How Do You Do?
     Mother Speaks About Turning Winter Into
        a Tree of Life

4   Trying to Trust Myself 33
     We Were a Circle Once
     Bird of Witness
     The Faceless Day

5   Early Days of Marriage 44
     In the Back of My Mind,
     My Brother David and the Dream

6   Releasing Troubling Memory 59
     A Man Waits to Be Married

7   Beyond Faultline 74
    February Faultline
    Settled
    Early Childhood Photo Taken by Our Father

8   Fire, Gift of Metaphor 83
    First Star
    What the Body Knows
    Rooster
    Gift of Fire
    Estuary: The Snake River, Maine

9   Extending My Reach 95
    At the Children's Bereavement Center of South Texas

10 Piecing David's Life Together 104
    Indigo

Part Two:
Voice

    Levitation

11 Haiku Healing 127

12 Voice Speaks Through Dreams and Poems 137
    Vision
    Two Faces, One Name
    Why My Former Pastor Sent Me a Letter of Reprimand
    Cain Tries to Explain
    Cain and Abel's Sister
    Swimming the Frio Near the Headwaters
    Winter Swimming
    Quiet House Epiphany

13 Becoming Owl-Woman 163
    Owl-Woman Dream
    Scientist of Silences

Stem
Where Does the Circle Begin?
These Spirals that Surge
In the Classroom Next to Assumption Chapel

14 Swimming as Means of Reconnecting the Split Self .. 191
I Listen by Covering My Ears with a Swim Cap
The Water Ahead Is Cold

15 David's Hair and His Childhood Diary, 1963 196
Looking for My Brother's Hair
Unfilled Pages

16 David Speaks: An Extended Monologue 203
Golden Octopus: Reconnection

Afterword: Dear David 227
Listening for Owl

References 233

Acknowledgments 235

About the Author 241

Preface

December 12, 2024

Dear Reader,
I am honored that you are here, that you are willing to travel this journey of memory, forged into poems and prose. Thank you for being open and curious. Thank you for trusting me as your storyteller.

It is my deep desire that *Words Make a Way Through Fire* serves as a healing presence in the world. This book is unique for how it faces profound human struggle, family trauma, and the aftermath of teenaged suicide by offering an integration of narrative prose, poems, and journal entries that document my gradual recovery from bearing traumatic witness. This interweaving of poetry and narrative prose serves as the body of the book because writing poems and keeping a journal played a crucial role in facilitating my process of psychological integration. Expressive writing has tremendous therapeutic potential and power, especially for individuals living the reverberations of traumatic events.

Because of the healing spirit of this book, I want you to be prepared for a disturbing account you will encounter in an early chapter. This is a story about living creatively with memory infused with the sensory details of seeing, hearing, and smelling my eldest brother David's suicide—the whirlpool of tangled, confused, charged feelings that accompanied such witness. David chose a method for ending his life that was not immediately fatal for him, nor painless. It was vivid, terrifying, and messy. It involved fire.

It is important that you are not caught unaware of this when you enter the story, especially if you have a history of trauma in your own life. It is important to me that you are informed and take care of yourself as you read.

Chapter 2 is where I narrate thoroughly what I observed and experienced when David, age nineteen, mortally wounded himself on a Friday night in February 1974 at our family home in Cincinnati, Ohio. This way of wounding himself was excruciating for him; it damaged every inch of skin and devastated his lungs. What I perceived, felt, and heard during those endless moments is seared into my body and soul.

In order to function as I tried to help him, I had to dissociate. A split took place within me; a degree of feeling left my body. Waves of helplessness engulfed me as waves of fire engulfed David. My sense of self as whole and trustworthy, tentative at age sixteen, was shattered that night.

At first I was mostly shocked and horrified. Then, guilt and confusion overtook me, along with numbness. It was years before I could grieve.

Writing poems and journaling helped me to find a healing path. I discovered that writing poems, including revision as craft and as a spiritual process that deepened my inward listening and facilitated psychological integration, allowed me to piece a coherent, trustworthy sense of self back together. One poem at a time. Gradually. There were times when I could feel expansiveness and an easing of emotional pain take place as I wrote a poem. This lifted my spirit and enlarged my courage and capacity to feel.

Language, especially stories and poems, have been a source of vitality and connection for me since childhood. I was blessed

Preface

with parents who read aloud to their children and told invented stories. Their animated voices as they read or told stories stimulated my imagination and inner sight. Their voices created dramatic and hopeful worlds. Wove me into a family circle that I shared with my three brothers. No wonder I have felt called to write since I was a small child—drawn to write poetry, to keep a journal, and to dream-tend.

Thus, this telling is *most* about rediscovering my innate wholeness with poetry as a lifelong companion. This book focuses on the healing of my heart and soul, a journey centered on learning to trust my instincts—my inner guide, whom I came to call Voice. The more that I attended to poems surfacing in me, the more I heard the quiet, luminous voice alive within, one that intends my highest good. The more poems that surfaced in me, the more I felt befriended by and able to align with healing energies.

Voice was present the night of David's suicide. Voice made a promise to me then, which became fulfilled over the course of many years. Voice is my word for the creative, loving, sacred reality that holds together my human existence and the larger world that I know. It encompasses the natural world and the cosmos, as well as the realm of those who have died. Voice often leads me to write poems that have powerful, expansive effects upon me.

In this book, I try to explain *how* particular poems generated such transformative, healing energy. This fascinates me.

As best I can, I want to understand how these healings, these psychological and spiritual transformations, arise and ripple from the wordplay, from the sensory specifics, the lyrical lines, rhythms, and metaphorical frameworks of poems. I want to understand as best I can *how* poetry can serve as medicine, and *how* language can cultivate our wellness and our recovery from emotional wounds, especially from traumatic experiences.

What To Make of Poems That Help Tell This Story

You will find my poems throughout each chapter. They are integral to my creative journey and to my recovery; therefore, they are integral to my storytelling. I couldn't do this any other way, any more than a swimmer could swim without the ocean or lake, or a basketball player could play without a ball.

If you are not accustomed to poems telling you a story, you might feel a bit unsure. Regrettably, many people in our culture have little exposure to poetry. Please know that we all speak poems often without realizing it: when we describe an experience about which we care strongly, and which makes a powerful impression on our senses. Poems are a natural form of human speech, of human storytelling, an expression of human feeling. It is easy in our culture to forget this. Perhaps you will rediscover this important truth as you read *Words Make a Way Through Fire*.

Think about musicals that appeal to you—how the songs reveal the inner lives of main characters in the story, reveal where the characters stand and how the ground beneath them feels, how the songs highlight key moments and turning points and profound realizations. Poems are like those songs, sung with only the incredible instrument of the human body.

Think of this book as a musical without an apparent orchestra.

Words Make a Way Through Fire

Allow yourself to read my poems aloud! Feel the words vibrate as they move through your mouth. Feel them resonate in your body. Let the vowel sounds have an emotional effect on you. In this way, you can better hear the music embedded within the poetic lines. You will become the singer without a musical score.

Trust that you don't need to "get" everything in the poem to receive something important from it. It is enough to be aware of the feelings that the poem stirs in you. Try to notice how my poems make you feel. Try to notice the sensations that they create in your body, and the images that they generate in your imagination.

Simply be open to them. Trust yourself and trust them.

For many years, I have carried the persistent need to tell this story. This means that I have carried a need to discern the truest nature of the story working deeply within me. Yes, I have carried the imprint of the night of David's suicide in my body and soul for fifty years. *And* I have carried the miraculous vibration of Voice speaking from the mirror that night, and through subsequent years, helping me to write poems that reconstructed my wholeness.

While my ongoing recovery and spiritual growth is not finished, the telling of this story is settled. It has finally found its truest words, its deepest story following twenty-seven years of discernment. Thank you for entering into my journey and for receiving my experiences, my words.

And, if as you read, your own flow of words emerges, alive with memory and feeling, asking to be formed into poems or paragraphs, please stop reading. Listen to what wants to be spoken or written from within you. Let your inner river of images and feelings speak. Write your words down! The pages of *Words Make a Way Through Fire* will wait for you. Your story too is sacred, necessary, whispering.

Sincerely,
Cyra Sweet Sanborn Dumitru

My Brother's Cup

Amidst chipped porcelain and stained coffee mugs
stacked in Mother's cabinet, glints my brother's silver cup.

I reach for it, follow his engraved name
and date of his birth with my finger, pause—

memory of his self-inflicted death flares. Settles.
It is good to find you here after years of reckoning.

I open the water, rinse away traces of dust, fill
my brother's cup. The water I drink now is cool and clear.

Part One

My Brother David and the Dreams

Chapter 1

The Grounding of Water in Early Childhood

Greenwich Point, Connecticut, 1961

> Ocean fills my child-sight
>   flows forward, forward
>   Waves tumble and vanish,
>   fall back into the gleaming—
>   surge forward again
>   breathing in and breathing out . . .
>   Is that my name
>   sounding upon the wind?

Constant movement of waves reaches me—splashes over small bare feet, smoothing then unsettling the sand where I stand. The wave ends, the ocean seems to end. But then, the broken wave regathers and slides back, back into the larger shining body that goes on forever, fills all that I see.

Everything before me breathes, cascades, gleams. Breaks and remakes itself.

Feel of Mother's hand, warm sound of her voice as she calls to my two older brothers running into the waves—swimmers

Words Make a Way Through Fire

already. They disappear into the glistening expanse then surface, laughing and splashing. My younger brother drops behind me into the sliding foam, clutches a sleek strand of seaweed.

Waves ripple toward me. Can I outrun them as they chase me? Can I turn and chase them back to the ocean?

Sometimes when we arrive at the beach, the sea looks far away, as if considering its depths privately, whispering to itself. I can walk and walk the wet sand without holding anyone's hand. Other times, the sea roars up the beach, shouting out its story; mesmerized, I watch and listen.

Here is origin, where I begin, within and alongside the ocean, place of momentum and rhythms of language.

Place of wholeness as if the sounding ocean holds the horizon and all of us together.

Place of first knowing that I belong to a body called family.

Here is the imprint of voice—voice of Mother reading stories and poems aloud by summer's day. At night, there is voice of Father inventing stories around a campfire. Always in the background breathe the unfurling waves along the shore.

Here is power of circle, being part of a family circle gathered for meals, campfires, and listening to stories after swimming the shining, tugging sea.

Here my body discovers pull of tides and currents—learns how to swim.

The ocean is both perfection and danger: alive and summoning me into its depths, where gentleness of current swirling at my ankles becomes stronger, hitting me in the knees and overwhelming me suddenly when the sand falls away.

The world is pure wave carrying me into the distance, away from everything solid and familiar, away from everyone who knows my name. For a measureless moment I am lost. Until another wave sweeps me toward shore, where I find ground again.

The Grounding of Water in Early Childhood

These are the days of my early childhood. For three years, until I was six, my family lived in Old Greenwich, Connecticut, spending summer months at the beach. Awareness first rooted in me here, through my body's immersion in the ocean and through listening to stories.

Because of my parents, poems and stories are deeply linked for me with love and breath, with spaciousness and imagination. They are still a means of connection and survival, a means of receiving and comprehending experience, a means of enlarging awareness.

During these years I began elementary school, learned to read and to form letters of the alphabet with my own hand. During these years I wrote my first poem and understood on a level that couldn't yet be spoken that writing, like the ocean, was immensely powerful. I recognized that words carefully chosen could bring things to life, not only in my imagination but also in the palpable world. Words changed the world.

Everything that has followed in my life flows from this beach, this listening, this absorption, vibration of words and waves, venturing into watery depth, learning my letters—this brief but vital grounding time.

As I look back from the vantage point of many years, I see that this is where I learned to witness. I learned to watch and behold the sea first by standing alongside it and then by swimming its currents. I discovered the sight inside my mind by listening to poems and stories. I discovered I could become part of the waves and be filled with images made from words.

Waves and words, breaking and remaking, watching and listening, the body's sensations and powerful inward sight, the human voice merging with the ocean's rhythm, all became inextricably linked. All became the ground I could finally stand strong upon, years following that reverberating night in February.

Words Make a Way Through Fire

Revisiting a Childhood Beach When I Am Fifty

One step into this sand,
and I am water sliding into water,
sliding back into depth
while I hold the sky.

Stories told in my mother's voice
ride across my shoulders,
tumble at the shore.
I grow legs and follow the words
follow my brothers
to a circle of towels
damp upon warm sand.

This is where the world first opened up
where I learned to listen.
While her voice made visible the invisible,
sand became another skin
became a hand to bear
our growing weight.

When the book closes
there is still the ocean to listen to,
the leavings of low tide
to examine.

As I walk this unwritten expanse,
a single wave rushes forward
sends a current upwards through my spine
dissolves bone
and I am water
spinning upright in the wind.

Chapter 2

That Reverberating Night in February

Cincinnati, Ohio, February 8, 1974

I am brushing my teeth in the small, burgundy-tiled bathroom connected to my bedroom. Of the four of us, I am the third child and the only girl. This allows me the larger room with private bath—formerly the master bedroom of another household. My brothers' bedrooms line the dim, narrow hallway just outside my room. At the end of that hallway is a larger, yellow-tiled bathroom shared by my brothers David (age nineteen), Noel (age seventeen), and Peter (age fourteen).

It is a Friday night in February, one of those discouraging gray twilights in Cincinnati. 1974. I am barely sixteen. Tonight, I am making ready for my boyfriend to pick me up in his Volkswagen Beetle and take me to a high school basketball game. I like basketball well enough, although my sport is soccer, and even more so, horseback riding—the peace of riding through wooded trails, hearing the wind rustle the high branches of trees, and feeling my heart's confusion ease somewhat. In this moment, what I like most is my boyfriend of several months, Brian. Perhaps this relationship might last through my junior

Words Make a Way Through Fire

year, I think, maybe even into my senior year. The idea of a male person who has room for me in his life feels urgent.

I am just about to turn on the water to spit, when I hear David screaming from outside our house. I spin around and try to see through the wide wavy lines of my bathroom window—an orange, flaring shape the height of a grown man moves through the darkening air screaming.

Oh God. He's burning himself.

I turn to the mirror, as if searching for a way out. In that pause, I hear Voice.

Cyra, this is going to be very hard! A part of you must hide, a part of you has to deal with what you are about to see. And hear. Smell. I will help you. Remember the dream I sent you a few days ago. Someday, all of you will circle back.

What is this Voice? Why is it calling me by name?

How do I know that my brother is trying to kill himself? That is what he did in my dream!

A presence splits off from the feeling part of me, takes charge, propels me into motion. We run out of my room and out the front door, just steps from my room. David is there—a ball of fire with legs.

"Roll!" I yell, remembering the classic advice. Then I realize its futility, here and now.

David throws himself into a shoulder roll, charring the small boxwoods that line the front walkway. Not a single flame is diminished. *Go get help*, Voice says. I run indoors, lock the door behind me, fearful that David will enter and set the house on fire. *Don't lock your brother out*, Voice says, and I unlock the handle. As my brother enters right behind me, I run down the dark hallway, through the kitchen and dining room and out the back door, yelling for help as I dash across Rettig Lane to the Mitchells.

My body won't hold still as I speak, "David, fire, burning himself."

That Reverberating Night in February

Mrs. Mitchell grabs the phone on the kitchen wall, calls the fire department and requests an ambulance. She pauses to ask our street number. I have to stand still to think. "7480 DeMar Road." Her eldest daughter Kathy appears and hurries with me back to the house.

What will I find? What will the flames have done to David's body? Will the inside of the house be burning?

Smoke billows from my bedroom door, and I follow the choking smoke to my bathroom. David had come here first to the shower nearest the front door and extinguished the flames. Large embers smolder in the Oriental rug in my room. I turn and follow bloody footprints down the hallway carpet to find David standing in the lime-green bathtub. Water turned off.

He is alive, standing up, mostly naked and bald—hair and clothes burned off. A few charred strips of clothing hang from his stocky frame. Smoke and scent of gasoline waft in the humid air. He mumbles something about needing his wheat germ.

I allow myself to feel momentarily. I am horrified by what he has done—by the thought of how much pain he has suffered. I slide down the wall to the hallway floor, chanting, "I love you. I love you." I want so much to comfort him, hold him. He looks utterly alone and raw.

Then Kathy's voice. "Cyra! Help me put out these flames. We need pots of water."

I stand up and dash to the kitchen, grab small pots and fill them with water from the sink. Kathy and I pour water onto the small fires that blister the carpet by the front door and in the hallway near my room. A larger flaming gash still erodes the blue Oriental carpet in my room. David had been fully aflame when he treaded there.

Kathy speaks softly to me, "That was good of you to say that to David. My boyfriend committed suicide too." I put

Words Make a Way Through Fire

down the small pot I have just emptied into the now smoldering gash, murmuring, "I am so sorry!"

"Have we put out all the small fires?" Kathy asks. The smell of charred fibers fills my senses as we glance around one more time. Then I hear the wail of sirens down the lane, stopping at my house.

A fire truck arrives first, then an ambulance and an Indian Hill Ranger with his olive-green uniform and round-brimmed hat. Some part of me directs the medics to my brother through the kitchen down the hall to the bathroom where he still stands. As they carry David wrapped in white on a stretcher through the kitchen, some part of me floods again with tears while another part of me answers more questions from the ranger, whose calm presence and deep voice keep my feet on the floor.

"I don't know why he did this! Dad is out of town. Mom and David argued—something stupid about where David should sit at the table. He sat where he usually sits, not eating. Noel called from Earlham. They talked. Didn't hear what they said."

The ranger telephones the downtown public library where my mother is conducting literary research and has her paged. He telephones the 20th Century Theatre where my younger brother Peter is viewing a film with Charles, a family friend and Noel's roommate at Earlham. Dad is ninety miles up Interstate 71 near Columbus; Mother will know how to reach him.

How can ordinary conversation take place in the wake of this horrifying act?

Part of me answers questions. The stunned part of me looks toward the kitchen table where moments ago, David and I had set down our dinner plates. Suddenly David had looked directly at me, his eyes dark with despair. He smelled of doom. Anguish whirlpooled him, sucking the air out of the kitchen.

I felt frightened—vaguely aware that I faced a choice. Do I

That Reverberating Night in February

reach out to him or turn away? I turned away and walked down the unlit hallway to my room.

Standing now in the kitchen, I answer the ranger's questions, feeling David's despairing eyes on me. Failure whirls around me—consequence of my refusal to enter further into my brother's suffering, consequence of walking away, consequence of my fear. I feel ashamed of my selfishness, my need to flee the turmoil of family.

I feel the first twisting in my gut: a huge tangle of guilt, shock, fear, grief, and horror. It was as if, along with the smoke, I had inhaled a giant octopus, its tentacles now wrapped around my heart and lungs and stomach.

The ranger arranges for Mr. Mitchell to drive me to the University of Cincinnati Medical Center hospital where Mother waits. We talk a little about school, my being a junior. He says how sorry he is about the situation, mentions the recent suicide of Kathy's boyfriend. Everything feels like a blur until I see Mother. We embrace and weep. Soon, Peter arrives with Charles. Dad arrives about an hour later from Columbus. My parents' eyes look blasted.

A doctor tells us that David has third-degree burns over 90 percent of his body. The gasoline from the gallon can that we kept for the lawn mower that he poured over himself had been well distributed. The insides of his mouth, his windpipe and lungs are severely damaged from inhaling so much smoke. He is not expected to recover. His death feels imminent.

A chaplain enters the waiting area and offers solace, a prayer. We don't encourage him to stay. Instead, we telephone Noel at Earlham College in nearby Indiana. He is stunned into near speechlessness by the news.

I see David once before he dies. Mother, Dad, and I stand by his bedside in the burn unit; he looks like a mummy, cocooned in white bandages. We tell him that we love him. He gestures to us with a white arm and tries to speak. Taking a breath, much less speaking, is painful.

"Save your strength, my son," says Dad. Later, we regret not hearing David's final words to us. Perhaps he would have spoken of regret. Perhaps he would have spoken about love and farewell.

After we speak with David briefly, Dad sends Peter and me home in a taxi. It is well past midnight. We hold hands as we sit silent and shocked in the back of the cab.

A few hours later, David dies in the burn unit. Our parents have a few minutes with his body before coming home to waken us, tell us of David's death.

Hours following David's death, Charles drives Peter and me to Richmond, Indiana, to collect Noel. It has snowed recently; ice gathers in patches.

I want to cry hard and unrestrained. I want to cry and shriek this horror out of my system. I want to be cleansed.

I don't feel especially at home in churches, yet they attract me. "Find me a church, Charles. Any church in Richmond where I can be alone. You can pick me up after you pick up Noel."

Charles knows of a small church near the outskirts of campus. He drops me off, then drives with Peter to Earlham College. I sit alone in a wooden pew. The air is cold and silent. I long for lit candles but there are none.

I begin to cry, but the tears do not heave from the depths of my soul the way I need them to. Soon I will face my only older brother, the one who has now become the eldest sibling, the one who was not with us at the hospital. I feel a responsibility to be strong and contained. There is still this lingering unreality. I am sitting in an unfamiliar church alone, having only hours ago witnessed my brother screaming and engulfed in flame.

What was that Voice speaking to me? Where did it come from? It spoke simultaneously inside my mind and from the mirror.

That Reverberating Night in February

It knew me. Spoke my name. It felt connected to that dream I had three days ago. The dream where I saw David riding on my yellow, ten-speed bike headlong into an oncoming car while I stood in Rettig Lane, watching. Its visual story of David harming himself deliberately and me watching felt uncanny.

When I had wakened, I knew that the dream was significant.

I had even told my friend Beverly about it. Now I feel the relevance of that dream like a lightning strike.

Was that dream a warning? A preparation? How did it know?

Why isn't Voice talking to me now?

Reality as I once knew it feels turned inside out. I am thoroughly changed, yet the surface of my life remains almost untouched, impermeable.

I want to dissolve, but I don't have time.

Charles will be waiting outside for me with my surviving brothers in the car. I am their only sister, the one who witnessed the self-inflicted wounding of our brother, who feels an unspoken and growing sense of profound guilt.

Charles has just pulled up when I step outside. I slip on a small patch of ice and catch myself as I walk down the stone steps. I have no recollection of what Noel, Peter, and I speak about during that stunned drive home.

Carol, our former elementary school teacher, dear friend of the family, flows out our back door as we climb out of the car, wrapping us one by one in her arms. She and her son Clay have rolled up the scorched rug in my room, removed it from the house. Her presence is comforting.

Later that afternoon we walk to a neighbor's home where friends gathered to feed and comfort us. After dinner I stand in the driveway with my good friend Connie. I catch a whiff of a neighbor grilling outdoors, and it hits me. Scent of fire on David, scent of smoke lingering inside our house. My face crumbles and I am about to wail. Connie grabs my hand and says, "Come on, Cy, I'll race you down the street!" I start running, grateful to be rescued from the tidal wave, grateful to have this loving friend.

Our memorial service for David the next evening is attended by friends and neighbors. Aunt Jane, Mother's younger sister, arrives from New Jersey. She gives me a pretty matching bra and underwear set that I wear underneath my black floral dress. For new beginnings, I tell myself.

My good friend Marie serves as acolyte. At the end of the service at Indian Hill Church, when it is time for Marie to extinguish the candles, one candle resists. From the front pew, Mother notices this first, points it out to me, and I nudge Peter. It feels like a fleeting indication that David signals to us.

After the service, Marie comes home with me to spend several nights.

Monday, I return to my junior year of high school, and Peter returns to his freshman year. Noel returns to Earlham. Mother resumes teaching high school English at Mariemont High School. Dad travels to New York City to offer support to his only sibling, Vicky, who recently admitted herself into a drug and alcohol rehabilitation hospital, following a near fatal incident.

A few weeks before David's death, Vicky had been rescued from a fire growing rapidly inside her apartment. It had been hard to rouse her, due to her inebriated state. Was that fire suggestive for David? Did the image of fire making its way toward Vicky linger in David's mind? Was there a magnetism about fire for him?

A week following David's suicide, I waken to a presence in my room. I am still getting used to sleeping alone again in my highly charged room, now that my friend Marie has returned

That Reverberating Night in February

home. Her gentle presence had been such a comfort to me, especially at night.

I startle awake, sensing David's spirit standing near my bed, as if he wants to tell me something. I sit up, peering into the darkness. A man-sized body of air ripples. Frightened that he might suddenly burst into flame, I tremble even as I strive to project compassion toward the presence. Perhaps sensing my alarm, the presence slowly fades as first light flickers through the windows.

Chapter 3

Immediate Aftermath

1974

In the middle of Honors English class, some odd thought that I want to share with David overtakes me. Abruptly, I remember that he is dead. I can't speak my thoughts to him. To keep from screaming, I bolt from the classroom, turn left down a hallway and out a back door where students smoke between classes. I tremble, unable to really let loose and cry. My good friend and next-door neighbor Alice, sent by the teacher, finds me minutes later. With her quiet voice, Alice helps me collect myself. Walks me back to the classroom. I apologize to the teacher who invites me to come by her office and talk, any time. I thank her, gather my books, and return to the crowded hallways.

I am preoccupied and distant, trying to recall what David looked like before he became a pillar of fire. A flaring screaming body is all that comes to mind. I don't want this. I push this image from my mind repeatedly.

Questions flood me. I hear little of what my teachers speak during remaining classes. How long had David been imagining killing himself? Days, weeks, months? If I had talked to him and not walked away that night one month ago, would he have changed his mind? Why use fire? Neither a painless nor

Immediate Aftermath

quick way to die. Why do that to himself? Why did I have to be the one to witness? Why do that to me? To our family? How dare he!

At the end of the school day as I walk toward the bus, I notice the strong sunlight of early spring. I feel the warmth and see traces of green lacing the winter grass. Realizing that I need this light, I decide to walk the several miles from school to home, rather than ride the bus. I need a physical journey to settle myself a bit.

My mind releases its burning questions as my body's walking rhythm soothes, takes deeper hold. I relax into the beauty of the shining afternoon.

I round the bend of Graves Road near the home of the family whose horses I saddle up and ride into the green belt. Carolyn Greene has been especially kind to me since David's death, encouraging me to ride more often, and offering to teach me how to jump. I think about absence—how it is a presence. The empty chair at the dining room table where David used to sit. Setting the table for five and not for six. The visual impact of David's absence. In the mild, greening air, a poem opens up inside me:

> Space.
> A place
> at the dinner table
> empty.
> Once filled
> by form, a young man.
> A family has lost a limb.

As I listen inwardly to the poem unfold, I notice a young boy riding his bike along the road. I recognize him as a neighbor of the Greenes though I don't know his name. He stops pedaling when he sees me. I say hello.

Words Make a Way Through Fire

"I'll bet you pushed your brother into that fire," he exclaims.

I am shocked by his words, startled that he knows that my brother has died, and died by fire. Troubled that a child would carry such a terrible image, especially about me. "You have no idea what you are saying," I stammer and continue walking.

The imagery of his words fracture my mind again; I feel as if I look outward through the slivers of a shattered chandelier. The octopus tightens an endless tentacle around my heart, my lungs, my gut. I still don't know how to process emotionally what has recently taken place. It all happened so fast, and so vividly. My senses are still singed.

Metaphorically, the boy's words feel true. At times I feel like Gretel from Grimm's fairy tales, a Gretel gone wrong, who made a terrible mistake and pushed the wrong person into the oven, my very own brother instead of the witch. By turning my back on David's anguish that night in the kitchen, I left him alone with despair, unwittingly pushed him toward the gasoline and matches. If only I could have said simply, "I love you. I'll sit home with you tonight."

When I arrive home and walk down the hallway toward my room, I discover that Dad has nearly finished cleaning out David's room next to mine. He started this process a few weeks earlier, searching for a suicide note or any other clue as to why David ended his life. All he found were clippings of David's long fair hair, cut a few days before the suicide. Dad wrapped the clippings in thick paper towels, set them aside in a box.

I pause for a moment in the doorway of David's room. I recall David, a few months earlier, sitting at his desk with a grim, faraway gaze on his face. Cigarette smoke swirling around him. Dad says that that he will be moving soon into David's room, leaving the "master" bedroom to Mother.

Before I can tell him how weird that plan sounds, he says, "I retrieved the rug from the cleaners this morning and put

Immediate Aftermath

it back into your room. I hope your room feels more normal again."

Instead of replying, I go take a look. Dad has placed the large blue rug in such a way as to hide the scorched portions beneath a chair. I am not sure how I feel about having this rug back in my room. On the one hand, I like its colorful nature, and yet I can't quite get the scent of smoldering fibers out of my memory.

We don't talk about the rug any further. My feelings are too immense and tangled for words. I don't feel I have a choice about the rug being returned. I stop seeing it before me.

That night, when I shower, I remember that David first doused his flames here. His flaming hands had pulled the handle as I do now, not caring whether the water that came out was cold or hot—his seared skin no longer able to feel the difference. Will David materialize again from the shadows, bolt through my door to the shower, or turn and come directly toward me? I know it is not a rational question. I am uneasy.

A lot happens within the next few months. I win a first-place award at the Ohio State Competition in Free Enterprise as part of the Distributive Education Program at school. I hear my accomplishment read aloud to the school body during morning announcements and feel happy that day.

I twist my ankle playing soccer and hobble around for a few days. Alice and I edit the literary magazine, collecting poems from classmates and contributing our own. Brian breaks up with me, saying that we had gotten too serious. I spend as much time as possible riding Carolyn's horses through the green belt, trying to soothe my jaded, lonely heart. I keep journaling, sometimes sober and sometimes while fairly stoned on marijuana. I stay busy as if being in motion tells me that I am still real.

A poem I write is published in an anthology sponsored by the Cincinnati Public Library System. To my thrilled surprise, it appears among the pages of the city newspaper, the *Cincinnati Enquirer*. Alongside Langston Hughes's poem "Harlem" with its image of deferred dreams becoming rancid and then exploding, I tape my first published poem on my bedroom wall:

> *How Do You Do?*
> Reaching over rows of chairs
> and inner distances,
> we shook hands with our eyes.

I know that I need help, yet I don't know where to turn. I consider scheduling a session with a family therapist that we had seen a few times before David's suicide. Our entire family had attended several chaotic sessions. While it was a relief to have someone from the outside attempting to understand and guide our overwhelmed household, the meetings were thick with tension. David sat near the center of the room. Conversation revolved around parental struggles with him. I blamed David for much of our family discord. If he would just quit being bizarre, then things would be better, I thought in my simplistic, judgmental way.

After one of the sessions, we left as a family to have dinner. David was so distraught that he walked out of the restaurant soon after we had arrived and hitchhiked home.

Perhaps David's suicide was partly a reaction to passions and oppositions swirling to the surface during those first meetings, conflicts that we didn't have the chance to work through with professional help. Perhaps if we had been in family counseling long enough for a sense of order and calm to gradually emerge, all of us would have felt stronger. Our family had no language for the inarticulate pain that David embodied. David had no coherent language to convey the pain and desolation he felt.

When I finally schedule a conversation with our family therapist, he is remote. I feel neither warmth nor empathy

Immediate Aftermath

flowing from him. He does not voice concern for my traumatic witness, nor does he suggest further counseling. I feel expected to bear my experience alone.

Eventually, I learn more about the last afternoon of David's life. That day at Mariemont High School where she was teaching, Mother had heard from a colleague about a medication available for depression. She had shared the news right away with David when she arrived home, watched him take heart. At dinner, however, she quarreled with David about where he should sit at the dining room table with Dad being out of town. David resisted her urgings to be positioned at the head of the table. He remained in his chair, silent and stewing, refusing to eat Mother's quiche. When Noel called from Earlham, David grabbed the kitchen phone.

Many years later, Noel would tell our parents and me that David had said he was considering suicide. Peter had overheard that part of the phone conversation too. Neither brother had believed David, so they kept what they heard to themselves. They did not bring David's thinking to Mother's attention, and they said nothing about it to me. Within half an hour of that phone call, David moved from suicidal ideation into suicidal action.

Our private hauntings cut deeply. Each of us within the broken family turns inward with our devastation, rawness of grief, and sense of guilt. We lack any shared vocabulary for how we are feeling. Alienated from ourselves, we are restrained with one another, although we do love each other, and try to console one another from time to time. We struggle alone, separate from the rest of the family circle, in our own ways and in our own time.

During the autumn months that follow David's death, I visit a few colleges as part of my senior year. One weekend I find myself in the bathroom of a dormitory at the University of Michigan throwing up for hours. I have eaten too many greasy egg rolls and

Words Make a Way Through Fire

consumed too much beer. As I vomit, I wonder whether I might be able to vomit up David too—at least my violent, guilt-ridden memories of him. This thing inside me, this octopus with long slimy arms constricting my gut and lungs, tightens its grip.

During these same autumn months, Mother hand-stitches a rug made from vibrant, woolen yarn. The design she makes is original: an autumn tree shining its fullest glory, gleaming deep gold and rich red leaves. In the background, bare winter trees stand along with a tall evergreen. From the left lower corner, near where you can imagine the unseen roots of the autumn tree, comes a burst of crimson and coral strands, rather formless. Mother tells me, "This is a burning bush."

When not grading high school English papers or cooking for her remaining family or watching televised football games, Mother has long strings of yarn—russet, crimson, coral, marigold, forest green, moss green, deep brown—draped around her neck. These vivid colors contrast with her thick ivory hair spilling above her shoulders, as she leans over the cloth canvas spread across the dining room table. For weeks, at night and on weekends, she pulls the needle through thick backing, ties a knot on the back, snips the looped thread on the front with scissors, opens the cut loop with her long, slender fingers. With each strand of thread and each knot creating a larger design—a tree of life—Mother makes her way into this unbearable season of loss. While she never explains why she feels thus compelled, nor does she talk about the loss of David as she threads and knots, the connection feels implied.

More than once, I recall her saying, "With grief such as this, all you can do is enlarge, grow yourself bigger. Try to hold it." Upon Mother's death, I find a scrap of notebook paper upon which she wrote, "I dare not know inside what made David mad enough to take gas and a match to the flesh we gave him . . . the loneliness."

Immediate Aftermath

In this poem, I imagine what she feels as she pulls those vibrant threads: her profound hunger for comfort, her need to make something beautiful as a threshold into this new life, this life without David, this life knowing that he killed himself. While I do not comprehend it at the time, Mother is my first teacher about how to live creatively in response to devastation. She shows me that it is possible to create a bearable future one mindful thread at a time.

Mother Speaks About Turning Winter Into a Tree of Life

What else can a stunned soul do—
believe in leaves, branches, hidden roots
make them real, give them texture, plant them here
    knot by knot
how else to live with such leaving: fierce
and unexpected—meteor scorching the lawn
on its way to blazing through front door
        through long hallway
                through kitchen and beyond

How can it be
that any room still
remains, how can such anguished silence
be given any holy shape

Lean into autumn leaves as foreground:
let them hold the embers
of his suicidal passing, his fire
that will never fully extinguish
long as my body remembers
his quickening, his milky smile,
his generous young man's heart turned dark

Words Make a Way Through Fire

Leaves take his fire,
transmute them into Season
       of beauty of beauty

Pour endless yearning for water
into evergreen rising in the background knot by knot
(will there ever be enough yarn)
near the orchard of barren trees
Dig-in, day by day
unearth one more breath
with each piercing of fibrous canvas
by thick needle wide-eyed with crimson or marigold
moss green, deep forest,
brown of sleepless dreams

tie of knot
snip of strand
pulled from the soul's chaos
rethreading, rethreading
make it so, make it so—mercy, make it so.

Chapter 4

Trying to Trust Myself

*Indiana University, Bloomington, Indiana
1975–1978*

At the age of seventeen, I begin college at Indiana University in Bloomington. For reasons I can't explain, the idea of being one student among tens of thousands appeals to me. I want to hide, hide right out in the open amid a crowd. Worried about everyone in my family, I don't want to be too far from home. Indiana University is just a three-hour drive from Cincinnati, and yet it is in another state—away but not too far to get home in a hurry. Get home in a hurry. Get home, in a hurry. Home?

I begin my college experience with high hopes. The new freedom and new ideas crackling in the air invigorate me: fabulous free jazz concerts given by serious-minded music students, theatrical presentations, and poetry readings. It feels electric.

I apply myself to my studies, then get stoned on marijuana during weekends and drink too much, finding myself in compromising situations with male students that I regret later. I can't take hold of myself. Often I feel as if I am spinning or floating, as if I have no solid ground inside of me. Octopus tentacles grip my heart, my lungs. Being stoned erases sensation, erases time briefly.

Words Make a Way Through Fire

I am successful at my studies; I am flailing in my personal life.

In early November, I call my parents to say that I will be home the following weekend, while Dad is still in town. During recent months he has been living weeks at a time in his childhood brownstone home on Garden Place in Brooklyn Heights, preparing it for sale. He has overseen the completion of extensive repairs and renovations, decided which family furniture to keep and which to sell, and auctioned off Granpappy's extensive coin and stamp collections.

When Mom and Dad both get on the phone with me, Dad drops a bombshell. He will not be in town the following weekend, nor for Thanksgiving. Instead, he intends to be in Brooklyn Heights, spending the holiday with a female friend, someone very dear whom he has known since elementary school. He tells me that she returned recently to her childhood home across the street to companion her elderly mother. Casual conversations between them have led to a renewed and emotional friendship. Dad would like for me and my brothers to meet her.

My parents tell me that they recognize their marriage is over; they feel mutual love and respect yet no longer the sustained bond of marriage. Mother makes clear that she supports Dad in his growing attachment. She makes a point of saying she does not feel betrayed.

The words are hard to hear. I feel betrayed. I am not ready for another person to enter our family. I had hopes that David's death could bring my parents back together, somehow.

Worried about how my younger brother is taking this news, wanting to reach out and comfort him, I call our high school the next day, and ask a counselor who knows me to pull Peter from class. "It is a family emergency, and I need to speak with him urgently." Knowing our family history, she brings Peter to the phone. Turns out, Mother and Dad have yet to tell Peter what they told me; I feel terrible about what I just revealed inadvertently, making the situation worse instead of better.

I am growing up, I am grieving. I am tangled in many emotions.

I want to hang onto family members before they leave me, one by one. I grieve the loss of my family as feeling intact, a feeling of loss that I have carried with me since the age of six. Finally, it finds expression in this poem.

We Were a Circle Once

We were a family circle once,
complete and continuous.
We gathered around a campfire near the sand—
the Connecticut beach was our altarpiece.
Sparks crackled from the logs like monarch
butterflies. Dad told us his stories.
We lived his childhood as well as our own,
splashing in the bathtub he sailed as a boat.
Home was a fur-lined glove, though even
then, shadows leapt in my room with
the slanted ceiling. Anger
had its moments too.

I threw scissors at Noel when he ripped
my paper dolls, striking the back of his neck.
David threw a rock at Noel who didn't duck;
Noel threw a kitchen knife at David who did.
Peter was barely out of his crib. But these
were more the skirmishes of children
than eddies of a raging river, balanced by
brothers bathing curiously with jellyfish.

We moved to Ohio. Dad stuffed his stories
into a briefcase. Mother spoke her grief

by hurling pots and pans in the kitchen.
David trained a parakeet to fly to his finger
then sit on his shoulder, but the older he grew,
the more he smoldered. I crawled into my wall
with the porcelain rose handle, and lit candles.

We drifted off into shifting angles.
And the wings of butterflies are folded
hearts, afraid to land for fear
of falling apart.

I am successful; I am flailing.

I finish my first semester with a 3.9 grade average. I receive a semester's worth of credits for work in high school, which makes me a sophomore when I begin my second semester. The idea of graduating in three years and a summer takes hold. Ultimately I do so, but I nearly sabotage myself along the way.

More importantly, based on reading my journals required for class along with various essays, an English instructor tells me that I am a poet! He recognizes this quality in me and encourages it. He urges me to register for a spring poetry writing workshop taught by a friend of his, who eventually becomes my first poetry writing mentor. "Take yourself seriously as a writer. You can make a living at it if you work hard enough," he writes at the end of my journal. I am over the moon with joy. Since the age of six, I have felt called to be a writer.

In high school, I sought out any extracurricular activity relating to writing: I took summer school creative writing classes and became staff writer, and then features editor, for *The Chieftain* (our school newspaper) and coeditor of *The Maize* (our literary magazine). My poem lamenting the deaths of classmates in car crashes was published in our senior yearbook. My poem that was accepted in a literary publication for children and teens

Trying to Trust Myself

sponsored by the Cincinnati Public Library System appeared one Sunday in the *Cincinnati Enquirer.*

During my childhood, Mother brought poems to life by reading them aloud with a playful sense of drama. I can still hear a poem by John Ciardi about a fat cat keeping vigil outside of a mouse house in the hall wall in Mother's meowing voice.

One day, when we were still living in Old Greenwich and I was staying home from first grade because of a sore throat, I got to thinking about a bluebird singing. It felt urgent to write what I was hearing and seeing in my mind. As I slowly formed my letters, the bird in my mind became real! Felt and present. While I no longer have the poem that I wrote that day, I have this poem that remembers being that six-year-old child enthralled by the aliveness of words.

Bird of Witness

When I was six, learning to write was first about drawing shapes:
circles and lines that looked like twigs fallen from our backyard tree.

It was about paying attention to how we filled space,
making our marks, learning to erase gently

so that we didn't tear holes in the wide-lined paper.
The weeks progressed and we connected the shapes,

forming the very letters that we had sung about as "alphabet."
We were makers! Tiny animals with spines and bellies,

tails and round heads, thrusting legs and rounded hips
sprang from our fingertips. They lined up side by side

Words Make a Way Through Fire

and vibrated the names of things: bird, tree, flying.
I had not seen this coming.

One day when I was home from school and feeling lonely,
the bird nesting inside my mind wanted a new tree to sing from;

it poked and poked my fingertips with its beak.
Find a pencil, find some paper.

I tore out a page with wide lines from my tablet.
I found a pencil. My fingers led me as I followed

the sounds stringing together an image from my mind.
Words whispered. Then it happened.

As I wrote "b – i – r –d," one blue wing –
another – then a small, sharp beak –

rubbed an opening through my mind
through my fingers into the kitchen air

until an entire bird appeared; it was blue and singing.
Perched upon a leafy branch, it sang and sang a blue

so real that my brother hurried into the room,
sat down and strummed along with his guitar.

    I knew in that moment that imagined birds could become living birds through mindfully chosen words. I knew in that moment without having the words to speak it clearly that writing would be central to my life. Written words had power.

When a university professor recognizes me at age seventeen as a poet, I practically levitate off the ground. A long-held dream is coming closer to being true.

Trying to Trust Myself

During my spring semester, I set my sights on a semester abroad in London. My poetry writing professor writes me a letter of recommendation. Yet, I hold back from applying.

I still drink too much, and smoke weed several days a week. I don't like that I have these habits. I see them as foolish, self-destructive habits that make me feel uneasy. Yet, I still can't get hold of myself to change.

How can I travel to another country for a semester and live like this? What regrettable trouble might I find myself in, far away from home? I don't trust myself.

I am battling internally. I can't quite name the combating forces within me.

Looking back, I recognize shame bred from a sense of guilt over David's suicide. I recognize how shattered I felt, how ensnared I was in the tentacles of unprocessed emotions.

This inner tug-of-war between creativity and self-destruction, empowerment and self-abandonment accelerates my second year at Indiana University. I slide into a disastrous relationship with someone older who turns out to be a sociopath.

There is much that I could recount. Suffice it to say that my desire for a stable, intimate relationship with completely the wrong person leads me further into marijuana reliance. In the middle of my fourth semester, we disappear to Colorado for several weeks. We return in time to convince professors to let me complete the work I had missed.

Months later, I lose a pregnancy through an early miscarriage. Interactions with the criminal justice system demean us both. I worry myself and my parents terribly.

I feel the pull of an unrelenting downward spiral, but my grades remain very good.

One morning, a poem arises and pours out a startling metaphor; it makes starkly clear how disconnected I feel from my better self. I feel empowered by the confident rush of words; the poem emerges intact, without need for revision. As I write, I pause briefly to enjoy the absurdity of talking to my face when I am headless. For a moment, I feel witty. Then, I read the poem aloud, and am deeply disturbed by what this poem reveals. I stand at a crossroads. I can either continue down this path of self-abuse, courting addiction and total loss of self-esteem, or I can begin listening, really listening inwardly to something life-affirming.

The Faceless Day

I awake one morning to find I have no face.
It mocks me in the corner.
I move to claim it. Like a snail
it creeps up the wall to the ceiling
and glares, upside down.
What have I done to deserve such treatment?
I try to cry,
but I have no lips, no tongue, no throat or teeth.
I can merely stamp my feet.

"You are too cruel to yourself," my face replies.
"I can't connect with you; I do trust my instincts."

I stand on a chair, yank down my face
by the hair and fasten it to my neck.
"We'll try it your way." But I can't move.
"I don't know what to do!"
"Write then, you fool," calms my face.

And in between the lines and loops of *W*'s,
I find a bug no bigger than my eyelash
who brashly swears it is my instinct.
Desperate, I swallow it. Goes down smooth.
There are no cymbals, no flashing lights,
just a whir in the shadows.

Trying to Trust Myself

How do I face this wild strangeness in myself? How do I face who I am when I feel fractured and traumatized through every bone? How do I trust myself when my decision to turn away from David without a compassionate word contributed to his death? How can I understand myself when I have lost any center from which to contemplate my life calmly and organize my thoughts? How can I gain self-respect when I feel stuck, deaf to my true self? How do I breathe fully with octopus tentacles wrapped around my intestines and lungs?

Where the hell is that Voice that spoke to me the night David became a burning comet in our yard? It assured me that it would be with me. Where is it? Where is comfort or healing or self-forgiveness?

The poem, in its wisdom, encourages me to believe—shows me—that good instincts live beneath my hurting life. The poem, with its quirky sense of humor, sees the best in me as a bug, a bug that can free me if I swallow it. The poem is like a dream unfolding an urgent, odd logic that gradually makes sense to me.

Reattaching my head to my body means trusting myself as a writer. If I can write a bluebird into existence, I can write myself into wholeness, write myself into becoming who I really want to be—creative, strong, trustworthy, and purposeful.

The detachment of head from body acknowledges the psychological split that occurred during my witness of David's fiery wounding. I recall what Voice spoke from the mirror: *Cyra, this is going to be very hard! A part of you must hide, a part of you has to deal with what you are about to see. And hear. Smell. I will help you. Remember the dream I sent you a few days ago. Someday, all of you will circle back.*

In psychological terms, I had to dissociate that night to make it through. An inward split took place, leaving a fearful part of me walled off.

Words Make a Way Through Fire

Writing "The Faceless Day" is a turning point. It reveals the wisdom of some voice within me. While I don't yet recognize this as my soul-voice, one connected to the Voice in the mirror, I instinctively recognize a saving voice in this poem. I recognize that I must listen to and trust this voice, enact its guidance when I understand what action to take.

The poem clarifies my choices and strengthens my belief in the power of my poetic self. Facing the uncomfortable truth alive in the poem stirs a healthier dialogue with myself. I begin imagining a way out of this destructive relationship. While it takes time to enact my extrication process, eventually, I see it through. Eventually, I stop reaching for marijuana to soothe myself.

I keep listening to the whir in the shadows, journaling and writing poems as honestly as I can. During the summer that follows my third year, I receive a poetry prize from visiting poet May Swenson as part of the 1978 Indiana University Writer's Conference. A month or so later, I graduate with honors in creative writing, a recognition based largely on my collection of poems, including "The Faceless Day."

Writing "The Faceless Day" begins what becomes a lifelong practice of poem-making as a spiritual and, therefore, healing practice as well as literary craft. Decades later, I discover the books of John Fox, poet and practitioner of poetic medicine. He writes in his book *Poetic Medicine* that, "You make a poem with words—but you also build an *interior place* when you write, a place where your *intuitive voice* may awaken and thrive." He says that, "Poetry creates a place for you to *live* your questions. Hearing or writing a poem works on your life so something new can grow."

As I write "The Faceless Day," I begin building a listening path inward to an unbroken part of myself. This path—this interior place—allows me to question my destructive self. It

Trying to Trust Myself

allows my creative instinct to gain voice and form. Through listening to the emergent poem, I touch spiritual center, and hear my trustworthy intuition murmur, speak insightful words that identify a way forward.

I start growing a new center to replace the one fractured by the distress of witnessing David flame, burn, and scream.

Writing can be a kind of sight, an act of giving my inward experience a physical presence—the poem itself—thus manifesting my reality. I can place a hand over my heart or feel my own pulse or hear my own breath and confirm that physically I am alive. Writing shows me who I am spiritually and imaginatively.

Building a creative path of sight is important because David's suicide is still the defining moment of my young life. I try not to think of him during my college years because, when I do, the image that prevails is David as a screaming pillar of fire with legs. I smell gasoline burning along the edge of his skin. This deeply embedded memory still resonates loudly with a life of its own.

My college years at Indiana University affirm me as a poet, troubled but striving. Could poem-making be crucial to fulfilling the promise made to me by Voice: *I will help you. Someday, all of you will circle back*?

Chapter 5

Early Days of Marriage

San Antonio, 1980–1983

I meet the man who will become my husband in 1979. In August 1978, I graduate from Indiana University, and return to what has become my father's house on DeMar Road. Peter is an undergraduate at Harvard University. Noel is finishing his undergraduate degree at the University of Cincinnati before applying and being accepted at Harvard Business School. Mother lives in her own apartment in Mariemont, the community where she teaches high school English.

Dad has sold 15 Garden Place in Brooklyn Heights and returned to Cincinnati. His relationship with his childhood friend has ended, and he has recently met Janet, who would become his wife.

Wanting to work as a writer somewhere, yet lacking experience beyond publishing a few poems and writing for my high school newspaper, I take a job as a secretary for a telecommunications grant based in the library of the University of Cincinnati Medical School.

It is there that I meet Daniel Dumitru. We are introduced at the circulation desk by Terri, who is laughing with a third-year medical student. I notice his kind yet strong hands.

Early Days of Marriage

I think his last name is an interesting word. "It is Romanian," Dan tells me. "My father escaped from Romania after World War II. He didn't want to live under the rule of the Soviet Union."

Dan and I see one another around, chat a bit. Then, one day he comes to my office accompanied by a fellow medical student named David. David sits in an empty chair and Dan perches on the corner of my desk, which is just inside the open doorway.

Suddenly, Voice speaks in the most direct and intense way since the night of my brother's death. First, I feel a powerful presence: an energy pouring from Dan toward me, strong as an incoming ocean tide. I hold very still because if I make any abrupt movement, the ripples might knock me from my chair.

Then Voice says: *Here is a good man. He has a really good soul. Your future is bound up with this man.*

I am stunned. No one else hears what I hear. Everyone else is acting as if we are sharing a normal conversation.

A few minutes later, Dan and David leave. I sit, unable to move. What does this mean? Why is Voice speaking to me out of the blue now?

I resolve to make a point of interacting with Dan, engaging him in conversation when I see him in the library.

We begin dating in early December as I turn twenty-two. By March, we are engaged, and we marry on Saturday, June 7, 1980. Dan graduates from medical school the next day. We celebrate my father's fifty-second birthday on Monday. On Tuesday, the movers pack our few possessions bound for San Antonio. Dan is about to begin a three-year residency in Physical Medicine and Rehabilitation at the University of Health Sciences Center of San Antonio.

We start our drive south in our two-door, five-speed Datsun hatchback on Wednesday; I am still coaching Dan on how to operate a car with a manual transmission, how to manage a stick shift and clutch when stopped at a red light on an incline.

During our two-day drive, I sometimes wonder what I have gotten myself into with so much change all at once, including commitment to someone whom I have known only a few months.

I keep reminding myself that if I still trust the call of Voice, then I have to trust this man whom I barely know, *and who is now my husband*.

I arrive in San Antonio as a newly married, deeply traumatized woman who needs to direct her creative energies. I want a new beginning. I want to commit seriously to my calling as a writer.

One morning, my husband tells me that he has dreamed about David. This strikes me as quite remarkable as David died before Dan and I met; they had not established an embodied relationship.

"He was in the hospital, all wrapped up in bandages the way that you have described. He said some things. He said, 'I love you . . . I am afraid.'"

Astounded, I ask, "Were any of us with him?"

"No. He was alone and thinking to himself."

I love you . . . I am afraid. I trust the insight of my husband's dream. These are believable words. It makes sense to me that David would reach out to me through Dan, send him a dream with specific words that he knew would be communicated to me. David had time to feel regret and fear of dying before he died. It comforts me to think of him feeling love for us as well, love for his family in all our imperfections.

I feel the breath of forgiveness in these words.

It is one of the hottest summers on record: a chain of century marks measured each day's heat in June. We have never lived beneath the gaze of such vast, open sky, a sky unmediated by the canopy of tall trees.

Early Days of Marriage

Dan strides off to work within a few weeks of our arrival at San Antonio Station Apartments on Louis Pasteur Drive. He walks there and back every day, crossing the street and the long lawn of the University of Texas Health Science Center at San Antonio. His professional focus and place within the community are clear. The first piece of furniture we purchase within the first week of moving into our apartment is a desk where he can study his medical textbooks.

I want meaningful work; I want to make my way as a writer in the world. I need to write poetry again; for the past two years, I have journaled only sporadically and written scarce few poems. The steadiness of my husband, along with his humor, honesty, integrity, and love, is an important safe space for me. Dan's disciplined mind helps me focus.

As I unpack a few notebooks from college, I find "The Faceless Day," the poem that I had written about three years earlier in a wave of disconnection. The creature in the poem urges me again to trust, trust myself and the process of writing on a regular basis. I feel renewed space opening inside me that wants to speak.

In the Back of My Mind,

a tree stands
like a young woman,
limbs arching
above small breasts.
She is unaware that I watch her.
Fantasies dangle,
sensual cobwebs between us,
strong enough to hold the wash.

For a few months I write daily, sometimes for hours, and often with a heaviness of heart that accompanies restless memories.

Words Make a Way Through Fire

"My Brother David and the Dream" emerges, the first poem I write that touches on the impact of trauma and my prescient dream. Something in me feels courageous, seeks to approach David's death from the stability and love within my marriage.

My Brother David and the Dream

You smoked unfiltered Pall Malls,
eyes fixed on your bedroom walls
trying to decipher.
On the other side of the wall,
I dreamt your dream:
I was outside by the lane
when you rushed naked from the house
jumped on my bike and rode headlong into a car.

Two nights later
your screams haul me outside
where you blaze like a lost comet.
No one else was home.

Our dream of death you made manifest
in the striking of a match.
Still shuddering from the stench of gasoline,
I try to decipher both sides of the wall.

During this time, David reaches out to me again from a dream. We are talking alongside a river. I ask him whether he had felt suicidal before the night of his death. "Yes, I had been thinking about it for a while." Then, he asks me what kind of work I am looking for in San Antonio. "I want to work as a writer." In his kind, big brother voice, he says, "You will work as a writer. You are very talented but have to develop discipline."

Early Days of Marriage

It occurs to me when I rise from this endearing dream that I need a dedicated writing space other than our small kitchen table. We find a recently refinished cherry desk that is spacious and sturdy. For an additional fifty dollars, the man who refurbished the desk, and his son, haul the beautiful desk up two steep and narrow flights of stairs into our apartment in 97-degree heat. We place it adjacent to Dan's desk in our second bedroom. That night, I write in my journal.

November 3, 1980

    I feel truly settled now, at home. I have my very own space—creative, working, nurturing space which I shape entirely myself. I have never had such an arrangement or feeling before. It feels exhilarating. I must become the strongest person I can possibly be and share my strength with others, so that others may discover the joy of a deeper sense of self and of living.

Within the first six months of living in San Antonio, I have a few temporary jobs and then find a full-time job writing copy for a small advertising agency. Through a circuitous path, I meet Naomi Shihab Nye, who is also recently married and working as a poet-in-the-schools in local schools and in schools throughout Texas. This work fascinates me, and I know I want to try my hand at it.

Naomi invites me to a private reading she is giving from her first book of poems. The audience is a small group of poets who workshop their poems once a month at Trinity University, the university where Naomi received her undergraduate degree. The poets receive me as well as Naomi with kindness and appreciation. When they learn of my sporadic habit of writing poetry, they invite me to join their emerging community. I eagerly accept the invitation.

Words Make a Way Through Fire

When I return to the group the following month, Carol Reposa reads a villanelle, "The Anne Frank House." I have always written free verse and am fascinated by the pattern of repeated rhymes and lines that comprise the villanelle. The content of the poem, too, moves me deeply with its repetitions of the lines: "The echo of the jackboots in the rain" and "Throws shadows on the tree that kept her sane." Just one word seems off tone—a verb.

When I mention the word, Carol lights up and says, "That word bothered me too. But I didn't have any other ideas for a replacement." The group discusses possible alternatives, and suddenly one of the verb suggestions seems just right. Carol is elated after she rereads the draft with the replacement verb.

She says, "When you have done all that you can with a poem, when you finally get the last word and when the last line that you've been striving for fits in place like the final piece of a jigsaw puzzle, there's a snap, or *thonk*!" The playful, useful concept of *thonk* enters my poetic sensibility. I am amazed by how at home I feel among these committed poets of various ages and various professional backgrounds.

The monthly writing group helps me develop a practice of poetry writing: deliberately making time to write, reading dozens of books about the craft of writing poetry by various poets, embracing revision as a process of rethinking how a poem communicates to a reader not myself, and giving readings. Furthermore, this community gives me a circle of wonderful, trustworthy friends: women and men of various professions who, like me, must process their feelings and thoughts as poems. They become my extended family; we reveal so much about our intimate lives through the poems we share.

Around the seventh anniversary of David's suicide, I write in my journal.

Early Days of Marriage

October 13, 1981

I experience various feelings throughout the process of poetry writing. During the initial writing, I feel awe and mystery. Where did this poem come from, and where is it going? I am a vehicle for the poem. Aware of its struggle for life, I seek to clear myself of will, surrender to the vision unfolding as poem. I am witness to the testimony and voice of the poem.

Later, when I rewrite the poem, I am more actively involved, critical. Now my choices are engaged. What line length and stanza arrangement is most effective? What flow of words and diction suit this poem? How best do I shape the body of this poem so its voice is clear, precise, fulfilled? Is this the exact verb? Can I strengthen the cadence without weakening the meaning? How best do I fulfill the senses of the poem so it is multidimensional? Can I eliminate an adjective or adverb?

When I read a poem publicly, I am a vehicle for the poem again. I experience a voice coming through me that is not entirely my own.

The urge to write is akin to the urge to survive. When writing I am listening to my many layers. It provides me with a stronger sense of self, and a firmer grip on my world.

I am immersed in poetry, upheld by poetry and by an ever-increasing circle of poet friends. At a weekend writing workshop led by visiting poet Ellen Bass, I meet Barbara Stanush, and we become instant friends. Barbara lives nearby with her family. We begin carpooling together to the monthly poetry group and to various poetry gatherings.

Barbara's husband and prose writer Claude Stanush had recently helped to form the Artist Alliance whose purpose is to

Words Make a Way Through Fire

organize people from all the arts, thus increasing our collective influence in the rapidly expanding city. The Alliance holds cultural events and has a publication called *The Revue*; eventually, I serve as poetry editor for the monthly paper. Book signings, poetry readings, and theatrical productions abound.

New York–based poet Daisy Aldan comes to San Antonio to lead a weekend workshop on the value of journaling. Barbara and I attend together. I had never heard someone speak about the journal as a form of disciplined mindfulness.

"Every day, every hour has its story. Every day is a being," Daisy says. "The journal is a gathering of your essence, of your life with feelings and denotations of your path on this earth. In it, you should record your observations, experiences, thoughts, feelings, dreams, and powerful images. Journaling develops your will and your awareness. It is a free act that clarifies the self by allowing you to evaluate your own actions. As your observations about the world and your place within it become more articulated, you become more organized from within, and thus your life becomes more orderly, transformative."

Daisy goes so far as to advocate for naming a journal each time you begin a new one and dedicating it to some feeling, idea, or relationship.

I feel a pull toward inward listening and outward attentiveness that is liberating. Journaling, along with writing poetry, makes concrete the continuity as well as the evolutions active within my inner life.

At the conclusion of the weekend with Daisy, I write a kind of prayer in my journal:

> Spirit,
>   be a clear flowing stream:
>   hold and mirror for me
>   rippling images

Early Days of Marriage

I can detect
and reflect
in currents of words.

What begins to fill the pages of my journal along with observations, images, and beginnings of poems, are descriptions of dreams—many of them troubled. Recurring themes and images emerge:

> *I swim in a pond that seems fairly deep. The water is choppy but warm. A tidal wave arises, sweeps over me and lifts me high into the air. Surrounded by water, I can't breathe. I need air. Somehow, I tilt my head back and find a pocket of air. I breathe, and then am released by the wave. I swim to shore watching the tidal wave crash against a rocky shore.*
>
> *David is in our kitchen. He receives an electrical shock and goes up in flames. I move into another room so I do not see the spectacle, yet knowing it is happening next to me gives me a kind of sight.*
>
> *David is in the hospital recovering from a second burning; it isn't clear whether or not it was self-inflicted. He has a fair chance of recovering and is receiving oxygen. A storm approaches. David is on the top floor of a very tall hospital. Rain, thunder, and lightning engulf the hospital. As the storm subsides, molten clouds appear and pour flames onto the hospital. I rush inside the hospital and discover that a fire has started in David's wing. I chant, "Rain, rain, rain!" to start up the rain again, and it does fall, squelching the fire. Yet David dies. I go to him, weeping. Over and over I say, "I miss you, I miss you, I miss you."*

I wake to Dan holding me as I cry out.

I better understand my brother's pain and sorrow. He seems

Words Make a Way Through Fire

to live inside me even more strongly. Sometimes I also dream that he is alive, recuperating from his wounds and becoming healthy. Sometimes I wish Dad and Peter had not scattered David's ashes off the Connecticut coast but had interred his remains at Indian Hill Church and engraved his name on a gravestone. That way, I would have a physical place I could go to where I could "be with him." It can overwhelm me to think of David as being everywhere, and alive inside me. I wish I had more of a psychic handle on my brother's life and death. If there was a place symbolizing David's presence, it might ease the weight of what I carry that represents his death: raw memory of trauma. I need to sink my pain and loaded memories into shapes I can touch.

Some months following the tidal wave dream, I experience and journal this dream:

> *Mother gives me photos of David as he was being bandaged for his burns. They reveal his appearance step by step from a hulk of dripping, melted flesh to a well-shaped, well-wrapped mummy. Sterile white bandages define his face which is stripped of hair, eyebrows, eyelashes, moustache, and sideburns. He waves stiffly in his white confinement, waves us closer, waves to whisper thoughts not lost as ashes on a salty wind. I can't hear what he yearns to say.*
>
> *What a chronicle of photos Mother shows me—a chronicle of David's passage from a living death to a death that lives on—for him as new life, for his family as a continual burial and resurrection. I should be horrified by images kept buried in my mind, in order to preserve my sanity to date. At first I am angry at Mother for forcing me to confront these disturbing images. Yet, curiously, I feel David beside me as Mother shares these visions of his wounds. His presence beside me feels supporting as I encounter his wounds visually.*

Early Days of Marriage

A frame within a frame. A carefully contrived distancing. Photos of a death are not a death; photos of a traumatic death which lives alongside and inside me seem to ease slightly my sense of horror. Somehow, David's presence protects, comforts me.

I feel sick and somehow safe.

This is as close as I have come to reliving the images I suppress. What a strange paradox: Although these images have capacity for harm, I also sense a spirit of protection.

Safe? Perhaps the possibility of my reliving visually that flaming, screaming night and passing through it unsinged exists for me now. Am I testing myself with this dream? Preparing or encouraging myself? Or am I gnawing at my suppressed images with this curious scenario?

If not for writing poems, I would be struggling with depression. When writing, I feel such joy, liberation, expansiveness. I love the absorption of the creative process, one that is immensely spiritual, one that feels as if I am entwined with a generous and breath-filled spirit. When a poem feels fulfilled and finished, I feel peaceful.

I liken poetry writing to prayer. When writing a poem, I encounter a life force that responds as I seek it. Spirit and I find each other. Perhaps I should say, Voice and I find each other. The poem that emerges over time represents our interaction.

Following one afternoon absorbed by poetry writing, I go for a walk with Dan. I feel thin as a windless day, feel like the spaces between raindrops. My body evaporates. Only my eyes have moments of sight, yet my visions are connected, real. I don't feel empty, yet I don't feel full. I feel no sense of boundary between myself and the world. Everything has fallen away yet all remains present, like being caught in a strange fold of time.

Words Make a Way Through Fire

⁎

Recalling my interest in teaching poetry in the schools, Naomi connects me with the Texas Commission for the Arts which connects me to the Poet-in-the-Schools (PITS) program that sends poets into the San Antonio Independent School District (SAISD). For two years I work as a full-time PITS in elementary, middle, and high schools. I come to know my large city as I drive from school to school and witness the many faces of its beautiful children: Brown, Black, White, and blended at schools such as Page Middle School, Tafolla Middle School, Longfellow Middle School, Highlands High School, Burbank High School, Crockett Elementary School, and Burnett Elementary School. Speaking the names of the children and teenagers heightens my appreciation for the multisyllabic rhythms of Spanish.

I see how poetry gives voice to young lives, contains and shapes their thoughts, feelings, and imaginings. I see how meaningful it is to these children and young teens to write about their lives, and then to read their poems aloud—be heard.

I feel myself amid joy as the younger children delight in the sounds of words, and imagine themselves as various animals, landscapes, and colors. I feel especially attached to Burnett Elementary School near South Alamo Street where I work several times as a PITS and as a volunteer. This school serves the children from a housing project that would be demolished some years later as part of San Antonio's downtown renewal. Writing poetry gives them courage: Expressing their feelings and experiences into poems that their classmates and I listen to and applaud seems to energize them as they return home at the end of the school day to apartments infested with mice and without air-conditioning, where quarreling neighbors and drunken boyfriends can keep a child from sleeping much at night.

Early Days of Marriage

I feel the need for a collection of poems by local poets that can be used with San Antonio school children and available in the school libraries. I approach well-known poets living locally to submit poems for the collection; I organize the poems into themed sections and write an introduction. With the support of an SAISD administrator, the collection *Green Rain* is produced and distributed throughout the district, featuring poems written by more than a dozen San Antonio poets.

But I am not the one who leads *Green Rain* to full fruition; Barbara Stanush completes the project, because soon after I submit the poems for the anthology, Dan and I start packing for our upcoming move to Norfolk, Virginia. Dan has been offered a promising position in the new department of Physical Medicine and Rehabilitation at the Eastern Virginia Medical School.

I have mixed feelings about our decision to leave San Antonio. We never fully accepted the Texas heat. We miss autumn trees with leaves that change color, and even the blanketing of snow. We miss sidewalks—they are strangely absent from many San Antonio neighborhoods. Our apartment complex has turned out to be a rather strange place, complete with neighbors who dye their small, black dog purple, medical students who show up at our door to ask Dan if he will prescribe medication for their venereal disease, and another neighbor carrying a handgun as he angrily seeks the apartment manager. We are not sorry to leave San Antonio Station. Yet, I grieve leaving my community of poet friends, and the creative energy of the city. I have found a genuine community, and deep sense of belonging.

Just before we move from San Antonio, Dan gives me a new journal as a present on our third anniversary. It is considerably larger than the series of floral cloth-bound, 5-x-7-inch journals given to me by Dad that I have been using for three years. This journal looks more serious with its dark brown cover and wide, tall pages. I name it "Celebration" and dedicate it to Dan "who

Words Make a Way Through Fire

enabled me to repossess my deepest strength and with whom I create a unique life every day."

On the opening page I write:

June 7, 1983

I am excited to begin not only a new journal but one of different dimensions. The cloth-bound books that Dad generously gave me were lovely and easy to tuck inside a purse. Students often noticed the colorful covers as I bent over them, writing so intently. More importantly, their smaller size felt comfortable, the pages easy to fill. Now I need room to spread out my thoughts and feelings, a sign of growth and confidence. The journal has truly become vital to my life: a silken tether connecting me carefully, not heavily. Through these pages I can live digging deep; I can love and grow deeply, broadly. These pages are shores catching, holding my flow.

Chapter 6

Releasing Troubling Memory

Norfolk, Virginia, 1983–1986

I am swimming. Tall, tall waves move quickly toward shore. I take deep breaths and ride the waves, one by one, then walk out of the ocean. Night falls, and I climb a tree, attracting the attention of a huge black bear. The bear grabs my leg and won't release me. I imagine rather than feel the claws and teeth upon my skin as the bear hangs on noiselessly all night. I have a split perspective, both as witness and participant. The witness searches all night for someone who can help. She returns alone in the morning to view the damage made by the bear, which has now vanished, leaving behind a lingering presence. Instead, I find a giant fish, shining and barely alive, scraped of almost all its scales and pressing upon something unseen. I find a room with a screened window through which I can escape. I open the window, prepare to climb out. I am about to climb through the window when I realize that the bear could inhabit the woods beyond the room. Wherever I go, it will be waiting.

Words Make a Way Through Fire

What does this mean, this image of bear? Is it a play upon words, a psychological pun that is more verb than noun? To bear grief, suffering, terror. To feel the weight of an experience, an onslaught of emotion as a heavy dark fur that encases me inside and out. To live this bear, to have a sense of inner bearing even as memory latches on. To wait as I feel the weight of the bear's grip. To experience, imagine, and witness all at once, a kind of divided self that bears what has been laid bare. A self that learns to ride the towering waves, to hang on through the darkness into the morning light, a self that finally realizes that the only real choice left is to turn and face the bear. The key is learning to bear, to create out of the fearful experience and bear a new life: a child that rises vulnerable, yet fresh and rich with possibility, a renewed being who might find meaning in the claws of the original bear. It is said that the Cherokee people regard the bear as a great healer. Perhaps to be held by the bear is the only way to gain psychic strength.

I dream this dream a few months after Dan and I move to Norfolk, Virginia, where Dan becomes the medical director of an inpatient rehabilitation unit, and faculty in the Department of Rehabilitation Medicine at the Eastern Virginia Medical School. I land a job as a medical writer for the Eastern Virginia Medical Authority, which includes the medical school, partly on the strength of poems included in my portfolio, poems which the new director of the Office of Public Affairs appreciates. It is invigorating to work as a professional writer in a dynamic, creative environment, producing articles on subjects that highlight our programs: in vitro fertilization, reconstruction of cleft palates for impoverished children, family therapy, approaches to chronic pain, and rehabilitation medicine teamed up with trauma care.

One of the first articles I write focuses on teenage suicide, the third leading cause of death for teenagers in the United

Releasing Troubling Memory

States. My article develops into a series as I research the issue and interview multiple faculty. Preoccupation with the subject triggers grisly images of burning men. My nightmares resume, and I waken screaming. One restless morning, I write the following poem.

A Man Waits to Be Married

From all corners of the earth,
a man waits to be married—his body
scattered like childhoods of the dead,
his desire tenacious as a barnacle.
He wants to reclaim his standing in the family—
the eldest, the hinge upon which
the door opens and closes.
Since his evaporation into flames,
the door has stood ajar,
not able to click shut nor stand aside and let
morning air garland the entrance.
So the young man waits
and sends messages like ships inside of bottles
to his sister as she dreams.
She can't quite read the scrawling on the sails
for they toss wildly on the wind.
She waits and feels his waiting while
the earth swallows diamonds.

When I first sit down to write, I think about being married, and how David will never have the chance to marry. Then I notice how the poem speaks about my unsettling relationship with my brother in third person, rather than first person—how David becomes an unnamed *he*, and I am represented as an unnamed *she*. I don't consciously decide to use third rather than first person; the poem naturally flows this way, reflecting my need for emotional distance from violent memories surfacing as dreams.

I also notice how the poem repeats the verb *waits*, and how both the man (or brother) waits and his sister waits. How the man tries communicating to his sister, and she tries receiving his messages, yet clarity eludes her. I notice the man's need for recognition. After I write the words *evaporation into flames*, I pause, notice how I feel a door inside myself that is stuck between open and closed, with the faint smell of gasoline and smoke. I think about my dreams, and my internal unrest. Though my life is moving forward professionally, in a deep inner way, I am stuck.

During an extended weekend trip to Clearwater, Florida, I sunbathe on the white sand watching the waves flow toward shore. Dan is indoors, attending a medical conference. These months of establishing myself in a new job—in a new community—and writing about what drives teenagers to suicide have been intense. I miss my poet friends in San Antonio, unable to find a like-minded circle in Norfolk. While I am grateful for the poems I am writing, I long for a community of like-minded spirits.

As I watch the shining waves flowing toward me, childhood recollections of summers near the sea loosen. I rise and walk into the soft, calling waves.

It has been years since I entered any large body of water, indoor or outdoor. For the past several years, I have been running five to six miles several times a week, yet not with pleasure. At first, I walk slowly into the gently spilling waves, my feet feeling the packed wet sand. I walk to where it is deep enough to swim, and then launch my body into the waves. My spine stretches and lengthens as if fully exhaling. My arms and legs work together in unified rhythm as I swim across incoming

Releasing Troubling Memory

waves farther from shore. I waken to the fullness of my body, waken to the power within my core, waken to a new appreciation for trusting my inherent strength.

I have a curious breakthrough. My muscles and spirit cry out: *Yes, Yes, Yes—this feels so good. This is how we want to move in the world. Released for a while from gravity. Sometimes facing the current with all our strength, and feeling how we hold our own, even when the sand slips from under our feet. Sometimes flowing with the current, floating and being carried. Yes, there is fear about what lives in waves unseen and with teeth or stinging tentacles, yet more than fear there is this joy, willingness to trust. You know how to swim with and into and across the waves.*

For a long time I swim, lingering in the waves. That night, I sleep deeply and untroubled.

When I return home, I join the Jewish Community Center in Norfolk where I build up to swimming a mile, three or four times a week. Swimming is a marvelous rhythmic discipline for me. To swim the distance, I must let my body take over, and set aside my conscious, thinking mind. The repetitiveness of coordinated movement reassures my spirit. My contemplative mind engages. My body and mind strengthen. Swimming for a long while becomes a kind of container that feels safe, a space that holds me as I move through it, using my whole body. Swimming invites complete physical attention from me. It integrates my mind and body at least for the duration of my swim.

Another medical conference takes us to Seattle, a city I have long been curious about, the city where something in David snapped and never mended.

At first, I am taken by distant mountains, how their snow-tipped tops seem to float between land and sky, their shrouded depths as dim as the blue-gray distance. Then, as I am walking near downtown, a siren lurches through the streets and rips open memory. The frantic horror of David's death drops over me like a crumbling chimney. My body shudders. My tears will not break open.

I find myself drifting through Seattle as if looking for David, feeling his restlessness. While Dan attends lectures, I leave the Madison Hotel and ramble through much of downtown, needing the exertion of walking and the connection of glimpsing people's faces.

There are many drifters—homeless men and women who congregate in parks and on street corners. Some of the younger men have a softness to them, a gentleheartedness. Loneliness and a desire for human warmth ripple from them, and they are occasionally cordial. Perhaps the rigors of material and competitive realities have defeated them. I can't help but see a bit of David in them.

In May of 1984, Dan and I buy a home in Norfolk, adjacent to the harbor in a neighborhood called Lochhaven. Within moments of first walking into the house, we both feel a kinship for it, a deep reaching into us with a hold that won't let go. It's a two-story home with hardwood floors. What speaks most to me is the side room, a porch that has been enclosed so that it feels like an extension of both the home and backyard. Full-length windows look out on the teardrop-shaped side yard landscaped with camellias, azaleas, and pine trees. I call it the Green Room.

Living in our house feels more like a dream than like living in our real home. We hear the deep bellows of tugboats and watch lightning illuminate the Elizabeth River.

At night, I still grind my teeth and dream frequently of fire. In one dream, I am a young man who rides a faulty motorcycle. It keeps transforming into a lighter with a tall flame that burns my fingers.

It is time to remake the past, and with it myself. David must be allowed to become more than my brother the suicide.

Releasing Troubling Memory

I contact a psychologist who has used hypnosis to help a new friend quiet her anxiety. As I begin my sessions with Ira, I start a new journal, entitled "Toward the Space of a Greater Light." I document my months of therapeutic disruption in the pages of this journal.

August 28, 1984

I want to convert my painful thoughts of David into some kind of warmth and affirmation. My personal horror is imagining David's pain and lonely dying. The impact of gasoline and fire upon the human body. The violence he inflicted on himself—the disfigurement he underwent as part of dying and making a statement. Perhaps the poems I have written that depict disembodiment such as "The Faceless Day" relate in some way with David disfiguring himself.

Perhaps through hypnotism I can recapture happier moments I shared with David, playing Frisbee pickle or romping with Jason. The crepe myrtle we just planted in our yard I think of as being for David, something beautiful that can grow and blossom, that I can stroke and love. My neighbor tells me that though you may cut back the crepe myrtle severely, it perseveres, growing and blossoming. I love how early morning sun gleams white along its smooth bark.

I need to experience more love and affection for David to reduce the suffering of the last dozen or so years, to broaden my emotional perspective. I need to complete my view of him and not only think of him in terms of one moment, rather in terms of a lifetime. I regret not knowing him better. I miss him.

A black wind spins in me, hovering
like a cloud of charred wood.

Words Make a Way Through Fire

September 11, 1984

As of yesterday I am going to a psychologist with the intent of undergoing hypnosis and reliving my experience of David's suicide. I feel relieved. I don't expect this process to free me completely. I do expect this hideously tentacled octopus to diminish significantly and allow me energy, space, and point of view to concentrate on other matters. I am constantly protecting myself as part of me tiptoes around this wound. It's as if I am bracing myself for another tragedy, or straining my ears to hear if memory will loosen images and sensations that I am not prepared to confront. I exert as much control over my trauma as possible through my writing and the nurturing strength of my marriage. I have brought myself as far as I can. The wall still exists. Because I hold my images closely, the only way to free them is to articulate them, revive them detail by painful detail. I want them to become independent of me, go out on their own, have less of a grip on my present and future.

September 24, 1984

Ira's preparing me to relive the night of David. I have homework to do—practicing relaxation exercises. Last night, I experienced myself as a dragonfly: That was how my body felt after my mind drifted into everything around me. Then I found myself imagining my rib cage, my skull and arm and leg bones, my muscles and organs. I have been reading an illustrated anatomy book designed for young people—the images have impressed me.

I love the state of mind I enter during these sessions. My mind clears itself; images and sensations resound. I become part of the environment. I feel renewed and

Releasing Troubling Memory

liberated as I step away from the pressures and preoccupations of daily living. After about twenty minutes, I feel ready to return to my bones.

The first time I experienced this state, Ira guided me through it. His voice like a mist hovering gently on the outskirts of my body. A few minutes into it, he had me imagining myself riding a bicycle. The one I pictured was yellow, the very bike of my prophetic dream of David's suicide. I have avoided bike images since then or at least tried to see other colors. Other images included drifting underwater watching a stream move slowly above me.

September 27, 1984

I am thinking about what I learned about skin from the anatomy book. Other than worrying about facial acne or trying to get a tan, I haven't thought much about skin before.

Skin literally holds the body together: the muscles and the bones, acres of arteries and veins, and all our innards. It keeps water and needed salts from seeping out of the body. Shields us from harmful substances. Warms and cools us. If I could somehow slip out of my skin long enough to measure it, my skin would weigh eight to ten pounds. By looking at the empty sheath of skin you could see where my knees and elbows had been because the skin at these places would be loose enough to allow the joints beneath to bend. The skin along the soles of my feet would be nearly six times thicker than the delicate skin of my eyelids. And, of course, my fingertips would be ridged with a unique pattern of swirls that would echo the clouds or the cypress tree in Van Gogh's *Starry Night*.

Words Make a Way Through Fire

September 29, 1984

Yesterday, I relived David in the safety of Ira's office. Smoldering feelings, repressed for more than a decade, are released.

Ira imaginatively took me back to the night of David's suicide. I expressed much of the tangled and silently smoldering feelings repressed for more than a decade. I spoke of my fear of being sucked into David's terrible mood. Perhaps even as he was choosing death over life, my instincts for self-preservation chose life. The pain, fear, and horror reclaimed me. This time I did not shove them down; I let them rattle through me, spill, and spill.

Before we concluded the session, Ira encouraged me to think of David during a happy time.

Afterward, as I walked into the damp evening with the sidewalk beneath my high-heeled feet, I felt an unfamiliar space within me, an emptiness. It made me feel almost dizzy. My center of gravity shifted so much. I removed my shoes so I could feel the ground beneath my feet. I had just released much of the raw energy of my traumatic witness.

Most of the huge, black octopus has just crawled out of my psyche, out of my chest and gut, leaving an uncertain, undesignated, and unclaimed space. Before, what I thought was grief was actually my recoil from the horror of his death. I feel I am gaining control with how I live with a hideous memory; it is but a moment in time. Instead of being locked into the tragedy that occurred one night, ten and a half years ago, I am enlarging my perspective. Loss fills me. I can cry deeply.

Releasing Troubling Memory

October 19, 1984

I had not fully understood how much energy had been required to contain the image of my burning brother. I feel disoriented, emptied, floppy; I have lost a defining structure, a kind of backbone for my life. My own nerve endings are growing back, and I don't know yet how safe I feel in this new psychic space. In one dream, I am living alone, moving through the apartment checking all the doors to see whether or not they are locked.

Although I feel tremendously liberated, my initial sense of great relief and renewed energy has evolved into an intense struggle for true self-definition. If the recollection of my brother's suicide is no longer the defining structure of my life, then what organizes my inner life? What can serve as my new psychic backbone?

November 3, 1984

A gentle steady rain. I walk out into the neighborhood, leaving my coat and umbrella at home. The insides of my sneakers are soon squishy, the solitude of the dark cool rain shelters me, and the oddness of my walk pleases me. I imagine that the sky is the belly of a great creature lumbering slowly through the universe. I think how the raindrops are lived moments cascading from out of our lives, being shed as people move through time. I think, *Wouldn't it be nice when I die to have my life wash gently over the world?* Thunder rumbles distantly, resounding through every bone, seeping through skin to flash lightning out of me.

Words Make a Way Through Fire

November 5, 1984

I keep dreaming about homes.

In one house, I live with furniture left behind by the previous owners. I say to my mother that I am tired of not having my own things, tired of living with other people's things. Then I discover rooms I had never seen before. These rooms are far less furnished than the ones I know. They intrigue me and feel peaceful. The distress I felt at living with the remains of others becomes a discovery of what was always there but was overlooked.

Dream-image:

A burning man emerges from the wreckage of a car. While the flames of the car are extinguished, his hands remain gray and smoking. Smoke drifts from them. Everywhere around me small fires burn, forming a kind of circle so that, no matter my direction, I am confronted by fire. The man walks away from the wreckage, leaving me behind.

Later in the day I am alone at home and yearn to unloosen a long scream twisting through me like a tentacle. I hold back. Then I let loose. My scream rings off the metal lamp on my desk and slashes down the stairway through the house. I scream and scream.

When my screams stop, my voice is hoarse. My body feels relieved. I have no more room to hold those smoking gray hands.

November 16, 1984

As the fire was first burning through his skin, burning through his nerve endings, David felt excruciating pain—I heard it in his screams. Why did he choose such a painful way to die? To be engulfed by fire, swallowed by pain!

Releasing Troubling Memory

I just looked up the word *calm* in my *American Heritage Dictionary* as part of revising a poem. I found a surprise. *Calm* derives from a Latin word, *cauma*, which refers to the heat of the day. It makes me think of a resting place within the burning heat of day.

Perhaps, following the first shock of unbearable pain consuming his body, through his physical agony as his nerve endings were destroyed, David felt a calm, a resting place in the center of his fire. Perhaps he had a moment of peace—a detached moment of strange beauty as he gazed through undulating flames. Perhaps in that moment before he rolled, charring the plants. By then, he had stopped screaming.

God I hope so.

November 20, 1984

Greater than my grief for turning my back on my brother is my grief that David died alone in his hospital bed, perhaps unattended by anyone—nurses or doctors. When did someone realize that he had died? Did an alarm sound as he breathed his last? Did a cardiac monitor beep some dead flat line? Did anyone work on him, try to counteract his body's succumbing to deadly injuries? Was there a final flurry of activity, or did he simply slip into the light unnoticed for several minutes? Whether or not he was attended by strangers, professional healers, he was not attended by any member of his family. None of us held his bandaged hand. He did not hear the voice of his parents or brothers or sister telling him that he was loved as he slipped from this world. Oh, how terribly we let him down.

Words Make a Way Through Fire

November 29, 1984

I am coming to see that I must enter this loneliness.

At some point in our lives we all must enter this vast, dark place and stand starkly alone, unable to see our hands before our eyes, unable to hear any human voice, fully aware of the fragility of our bones, our blood, uncertain of what path will lead us safely into spring light. This is where I comprehend the desolation of David, where I comprehend the anguish of my parents, where falling all around me is the silence of every person suffering in their core.

If I am to be truly compassionate then I must stand here. Stand and be still. Feel waves of abandonment from head to toe, feel fear so huge that it becomes terror. Feel my legs longing to bolt. But nowhere to go, no door, I have no sense yet of direction. Terror throbs around me in the absolute silence.

I listen to a distant pulsing beyond the silence, the vibration of which I feel more than hear, vibration of ocean waves breaking along the shore.

December 27, 1984

I came apart yesterday, upstairs in our bedroom while Dan studied downstairs for his medical exam. I started sobbing uncontrollably. I turned the fan on so that Dan wouldn't hear me. My insides felt as if they were crumbling into grains of glass.

I thought, *I must go to Dan, interrupt his work. I need him to hold me. I don't know how to share this immense pain with someone I love. So much of me has been buried. And now I am unraveling. I must go to Dan. What if he can't handle all my pain?*

Releasing Troubling Memory

I walked down the creaky stairs. When he saw my tears, Dan closed his book and opened his arms, held me while I sobbed.

Now I can see that the last several months have been a progressive unraveling for me. Will I become so disconnected that I won't be able to put the pieces back together again? Did David feel this same great unraveling? Longing for coherence, for certainty? Did he feel the same great weariness and fear?

I grieve for the intact girl I once was, for the person I could have been if I hadn't been confronted by so much anguish and gruesome imagery. Who could I have become without the haunting of that memory? Who might David have become if he had lived? How do I live in the present without fear, without hurt?

I realize that I have never totally trusted; a part of me has always held back. Dan receiving me with such love and kindness and understanding helps me feel braver.

I am gripped by a process that must be like stripping furniture. You aren't sure what kind or color of wood you will find beneath your own layers. You don't know what kind of condition the original wood will be in. And you will have to spend many, many hours refinishing whatever reveals itself. It is a tedious, lonely, sometimes grueling process driven by my need to feel whole as well as a curiosity about what will be found. God, I hope the eventual restoration is worth this unnerving disintegration.

Trauma displaces, disorients, dissociates, disorders, dismantles, disjoints, disquiets. Undoes. Familiar ground is gone even if some details remain unchanged. *Un. Un. Un. Un. Un. Un. Disss.*

Chapter 7

Beyond Faultline

San Antonio, 1986

Two years following my hypnosis, Dan and I move back to San Antonio. We move into a split-level house full of windows and open living spaces, filled by the changing light and shadows of the vast Texas sky. We feel at home.

Dan joins the faculty in the Department of Rehabilitation Medicine at the University of Texas Health Science Center in San Antonio where he trained as a resident. With much gratitude, I return to my poet friends who have continued meeting monthly, sharing drafts of poems-in-progress. It is easy to establish myself as a freelance medical writer with my broad portfolio of writing, editing, and public relations work for the Eastern Virginia Medical Authority. We feel settled quickly.

It is February, the month that David took his own life twelve years earlier. I am not sleeping well. The counseling sessions with Ira released me from nightmares of smoldering people, yet I struggle with feelings of guilt and questions around fault.

Who is at fault when a loved one commits suicide? Or should I ask: What is at fault when a loved one commits suicide? Is there someone or something that can be blamed?

If my brother was feeling desperate enough to harm himself, was he really to blame? What caused such desperation? Depression? Was the depression really to blame?

What about the circumstances of his life? When he died, he was living at home with parents, and brothers, and his sister. Didn't we fail him by not showing him enough that we loved him, believed in him? I was the last person to be with David before his desperate act; I had smelled a profound sense of gloom and doom wafting all around him. Yet, I turned my back on him. What if I had spoken kindly to him in the kitchen, told him that I would cancel my date and keep company with him?

I can't shake feeling blameworthy, even though I mentally understand that depression took my brother's life: illness of the mind and soul. Amid his suicidal despair, he was both himself and not himself.

It is up to me to forgive myself.

I dream of an earthquake, awaken with the word *faultline* in my mind. When I sit down to write, what comes first are the lines: "Sometimes the earth / shakes with the taste of my dead brother / I straddle uneven ground / and stretch." Thinking about the physical reality of an earthquake gives me a way to represent my inward state, how unsolid within myself I feel.

I keep my attention on the idea of maintaining balance while experiencing the ground fall away, how I need to stretch. Then I admit to the poem that I long to hear David assure me that I am not at fault for his death. I yearn to wake on a deeper level, ready to live my life feeling blameless, free of trauma-related aftershocks—find some enduring inner peace.

This poem emerges quickly, pretty much intact. I read the poem aloud and add the reference to the San Andreas Fault. Giving the poem a title is easy. The word *faultline* says everything—it acknowledges the landscape of earthquakes and implies the psychological state of the poem's speaker—me.

Adding *February* reinforces the link to David, through the pleasing element of musicality, the alliteration of *F* sounds, as well as the multisyllabic flow of these two words together: "February Faultline."

When I read the revised poem aloud, I feel relief—relief that I have aired my long-standing feeling of guilt and found pleasure in making something beautiful from a hideous memory. My self-blame feels creatively externalized, "removed to the symbolic but vivid world of language" as poet Gregory Orr describes it in his book *Poetry as Survival*. Admitting my self-blame in the form of a poem lessens my shame and lightens my heart.

February Faultline

February,
a month built along
the San Andreas Fault.
Sometimes the earth shakes
with the taste of my dead brother.
I straddle uneven ground
                and stretch.

Oh, to sleep February straight
through, to become
a still horizon
just for a few hours—
no jolt to accusing light
by the telephone ringing or
the singing of utility wires outside.

To awaken with silence
and the calm words of the dead
still thick upon me.

Beyond Faultline

> To reappear
> having invented myself anew
>   and faultless,
>   believing in deep places of rest.

I bring "February Faultline" to my graduate poetry writing workshop at the University of Texas at San Antonio a few days later. My peers comment on how the spacing between stanzas as well as the placement of several lines ("and stretch," "and faultless") create a visual impression of the ground shifting. This had emerged naturally in my first draft, and I decide on keeping the unsettling effect generated by the spacing.

The poem serves as an important psychological transition; it signals my readiness—as well as my desire—to claim a new definition of what it means to be a survivor of traumatic witness. I want to feel more secure, more grounded internally, rather than feeling at the mercy of unpredictable currents and triggers linked to trauma that is acknowledged, yet not fully processed.

Soon after, a dream arises in me that has an unprecedented tone.

> *David has gained fame for creating something beautiful and significant. He is returning from a long, long trip during which he received an award for his creation. I meet him at the airport. He approaches as a grown, healthy man who smiles broadly when he sees me. Overcome by this joyful sight, I cover my tearful eyes with my hands, and drop to my knees as David makes his way toward me. David's smile feels like an expression of forgiveness, implied by the delight and sheer love he radiates toward me.*

This dream heralds a crucial shift in my psychic relationship with my brother. A befriending process with David's memory

Words Make a Way Through Fire

begins. Having yielded to the disturbing images connected with David's death, I am open to receiving other images of him, such as reunion at an airport. Other healing dreams follow, several of which take place at the beach in Greenwich Point, where we spent our childhood summers before moving to Ohio.

> *David and I are at the beach talking, following a long separation. I mostly talk while he listens. I tell him that the imagery of his death has been hard for me to absorb. I mention a specific image of the stumps of arms emitting smoke. The smoke diminishes as I speak. Then, David's gentleness pervades the dream, along with sound of the waves tumbling. The affection I experience in the dream carries over into daylight. I waken feeling happy and restored, as if I experienced this dream imagery on a cellular level. I make new memories with my brother.*

David's spirit, I believe, feels my need for healing and reaches out to me. I believe that the spirits of those we love who have died can assist us if we are open to them. Perhaps helping us to heal frees their spirits on a deeper level.

Settled

They are still with us. Turkey buzzards glide
in and out of view, their shadows streak the trees.
Scanning the ground, these long-winged birds ride
the sky. Even their sharp eyes cannot see
you, gone sixteen years, your ashes exchanged
for the silent dust. This morning I dreamed
the old dream, yet it too was changed—
the flames died down instead of spreading screams.
Even the restless know when they find home.

Beyond Faultline

Buzzards roam a certain territory,
leaves follow invisible paths when blown.
At last you are free, no longer circling
or keeping a brother's eye on my grief.
We live in the long lift of memory.

Gradually my relationship with David lightens, expands as the poems that I write and the dreams that I dream reframe my connection to my brother. Other childhood memories surface involving David, memories that had been stifled by traumatic memory. I regain the fullness of David's life, moving beyond the disturbing nature of his dying.

While peeling pearl onions, I notice how easily the thin outer layer, the papery skin, peels off and sticks to my fingers. Suddenly, I recall how I had peeled fragile strips of David's blistered skin off his sunburned shoulders that summer long ago in Europe.

During the summer of 1969, our parents took us traveling throughout Europe for six weeks; I was eleven and David was fourteen. We stopped at a beach for an afternoon swim on our way to Italy. David was the fair-skinned child in the family. When we spent a summer afternoon swimming, he would easily sunburn while the rest of us tanned.

My three brothers ran eagerly to the waves while I sat on a towel in my yellow one-piece bathing suit with the black buttons. There were mostly boys frisking in the surf.

"Why don't you go for a swim?" my parents asked.

"I'd rather sit here for a while."

I loved swimming, but without my glasses I had little range of vision. With glasses on, I observed, let my skin soak in the salty air and the easy sea breeze. My brothers stuck loosely together; I gauged how far they were from shore and my parents. The other children, although a bit curious about my brothers, clustered among themselves. Eventually, I trusted my grasp of the larger context, the one which dissolved every time I removed my glasses. Feeling more courageous, I took off my "eyes" and dashed to the salty water. At first, I stuck close to shore before deciding to risk the waves with my brothers. Before long, I was aware of boys swirling nearby. One of them swam around me and then between my legs. I heard giggling, incomprehensible German words, and felt strange male presences circling nearby. Peter came over to see what was going on, but I didn't feel safe. Not knowing how to hold my own ground and mistrusting their intentions, I retreated to the beach to make sandcastles. In that moment, I wanted to be a boy, free to move about the world.

David was sunburned when we left that beach in Italy. His shoulders and back were bright red by the evening and must have throbbed the next day. A few days later, his skin started peeling. I recall how it tore easily in my fingers as I pulled the strips slowly, gently—the skin itself feeling weightless, flimsy like dried sea foam. All these years later, it reminds me of the thin, flaky sheath around pearl onions.

Another memory particularly soothes my mind and heart. The four of us kids had been raking leaves all Saturday morning. It was late in the autumn season, and the fallen leaves were wet and heavy. We raked and raked, carried countless soggy piles to a huge compost heap inside "the fort." Finally, Mother called us in for lunch. Then we returned to our rakes and our grumbling. Grumbling led to bickering, which led to serious disputes among siblings. David got sentenced to finishing the raking alone. Noel, Peter, and I were happy to be freed of the chore. Yet, once inside, I found myself unable to concentrate on the latest copy of *Mrs. Piggle Wiggle*, recently brought home from the library. I kept looking out the window at David laboring alone in the side yard. It didn't feel fair for him to finish that task alone. I laced up my sneakers, grabbed a rake, and worked alongside my brother. A simple, long-ago gesture now means everything.

During this time of reconnecting with memories of David's life as I shared it with him, I discover a beautiful black-and-white photograph tucked in a folder in the back of a desk drawer. It was taken by Dad when David and I were perhaps five and two respectively, one that I had forgotten. Dad must have been sitting nearby with his Leica camera as David and I sat side by side at a small table. We are revealed in profile. At first, I notice that David is in the background, reaching for something; I watch his reach. Then I notice that I am leaning my small head against the side of his head. In response to my leaning my head against his, he holds his head still as he reaches for a crayon or scissors or for something else. This moment of tender, natural connection between older brother and younger sister blooms diamonds in my heart.

This photographic image of our connection leads me to remember how on my tenth birthday David gave me a record, a single disk of the Temptations singing "My Girl." It felt weird at first, the gift of what I thought of as a romantic song from my brother. But I grew to cherish it as I listened to the words.

Words Make a Way Through Fire

Early Childhood Photo Taken by Our Father

At first it seems a simple study of two young faces.
David slightly out of focus,

as if he's underwater and radiating
one gentle tone.

Crisper light dusts my serious cheek:
casts a soft shadow along his brow.

Our eyes are not for our father and his camera.
What we are watching can't be seen.

White light splashes beneath David's arm
which reaches intently

beyond the edge. I am full
of watching. That is enough,

so I rest my head against his
just above where an ear must be.

It is this leaning.
David holding his head and me steady,

even as he stretches beyond the edge.

Chapter 8

Fire, Gift of Metaphor

1995

Twenty-two years since David has died, I am the mother of two small children, and about to complete my graduate degree in English at the University of Texas San Antonio, studying for comprehensive exams. It has taken me seven years to get to this point.

While working full-time as a medical writer for a flagship hospital, I could manage only one or two courses a semester. Becoming pregnant has posed years of challenges. Fortunately, Southwest Texas Methodist Hospital provided both sophisticated interventions to overcome infertility and employee health insurance that covered the cost of procedures. About halfway through my graduate degree, I set aside my graduate coursework to undergo zygote intrafallopian transfer (ZIFT). One ZIFT attempt results in pregnancy. We are cautiously thrilled until we discover during an ultrasound appointment at six weeks that my embryonic sac is empty. There is no human life growing inside. I had never heard of such a thing.

I grieve and grieve. Then I resume my graduate courses while working.

A few months before undergoing a second ZIFT procedure, Voice gives me a silent but heartening image of a future

Words Make a Way Through Fire

to which I cling. While swimming in our backyard lap pool, I suddenly see two fair-haired children about the same size sitting at the end of the pool, dangling their small feet in the water. I stop swimming and stare. Twins?

I enter into the second ZIFT procedure with high hopes. Two weeks later, I am hugely disappointed: no pregnancy resulted. After five years of hundreds of hormone shots and intensifying procedures, I am exhausted emotionally. No more procedures, I resolve.

Two months later, I become pregnant "naturally" with our daughter. When the nurse shows me the plus sign on the pregnancy test, I stare at it blankly, not comprehending. "What does that mean?" I ask.

"It's positive. You are pregnant." I burst into tears and throw my arms around her.

A few weeks later, ultrasound reveals a tiny heartbeat within the embryonic sac.

First Star

Imagine the night sky curved starless
and black, like the skin of an otter.
How dark the world below—
a deep and silent shadow
swimming in grief.

Now imagine when the first star
burned itself into the celestial sea.
How blazing its tiny beauty,
its unexpected light,
the advent of all stars to come.

From out of a silence that speaks
words we cannot always hear,

Fire, Gift of Metaphor

from out of an absence
that spins darkness into light
and emptiness into embrace,

you came forth.
Landed, took root.
At six weeks on ultrasound
you were a tiny star pulsing
the beat of a heart.

What once was empty now shone
chambered light within a dark oval sac.
Four weeks later we found that a body
shaped like a peanut shell
had grown around your heart.

It flickered inside your chest
like the smallest anemone.
As we watched the screen
you stirred within my inland sea,
stretched the small stems

of your arms and legs
then curled back into yourself
as if gathering
light for the next passage
the next great reach to come.

When our daughter is about eighteen months old, we return for the three cryopreserved zygotes, which are thawed very carefully and then transferred into my womb as embryos. One of them takes hold and becomes our son, born twenty-seven months after our daughter.

Both my daughter and son are born with fair hair.

Words Make a Way Through Fire

The responsibilities of motherhood form a kind of kiln, transforming my self-centeredness into a self-awareness that is more body-centered, feels more whole, as if I am landing coherently, solidly, with fewer psychic fractures, inside my body more and more. And, by landing more completely into my body, I am also hearing my instincts more frequently. Feeling my woman's power.

About a month before my daughter is born, my good friend Chris says to me, "There will come a time during labor when you feel your body taking over. Let it. Trust it. Do not fight it. Find your strength in this power."

Her words guide me as contractions come intensely and rapidly. At first I fear the contractions, think to myself that if they become any stronger, my body will explode. Then, I feel Chris's meaning, and I remember to trust, trust my own being on an entirely new level. I focus my mind and my calm determination to ride each wave, rest between them, and receive my own power. Holding my daughter for the first time feels triumphant and yet humbling. Holding my son twenty-seven months later feels just as triumphant and yet humbling.

Both the birth process and breastfeeding my children endow me with a new respect for the strength, grace, and brilliance of a woman's body. I love nursing my babies, fulfilling that fundamental need that our bodies have for each other as well as the tender touching. Middle-of-the-night feedings have an element of magic to them—the household quiet, and the material world resting in darkness. Just myself and my infant child: the latching on, the letting down of my milk, the intimacy which stems from hunger and nuzzling response. Even amid the sleep-deprived months that come with attending to a newborn, I feel present while feeding my babies.

Fire, Gift of Metaphor

What the Body Knows

I have been told by one well-schooled in touch
that the body has memory. Muscles recall
the terrible pulling away from fire,

shoulders curl years later as if still protecting
the chest, the cradled heart. Tendons
remain taut long after the smoke fades.

There are ways of touching that loosen,
unfurl, restore the ancient vein of joy,
give self back to self as well as to others.

For many days following the birth, I waken
from deep sleep moments before her hunger cries.
What travels swifter, deeper than sound?

Knowing unwinds a little more from my bones
while my daughter nurses. Her dark eyes
plumb mine and her small hands flutter.

Each day we move toward translation
as new skin begins to read like parchment.
Blue veins offer phrases and questing hands

fill in lost words while they grow past groping
to reaching, opening cardboard books
now within her grasp.

When I hold her, my muscles sing and all
that I know rushes to my hands. The swirls
in my skin listen and speak all manner of heat.

Words Make a Way Through Fire

With my attention preoccupied by two small children, the poems I write during this time are mostly about motherhood. To cope with our son's months of frequent wakefulness, I write a poem comparing him to a rooster; it softens my exhausted irritability.

Rooster

Born during the full
white of moon, you now
sense when the first warm glint

brushes the horizon,
even on thundering mornings.
Plucked from sleep,

you stretch, bob your head
and pull yourself to a stand,
arms pushing against the rails

of your crib.
In the early time
that lives before language,

your body speaks
becomes our first light
as we wake to your call.

You open wide your eyes,
tilt back your head
and crow.

Fire, Gift of Metaphor

❧

Then there is the day when I am reading a nonfiction book about trees aloud to my children when I come upon this statement: "Some eucalyptus seeds develop inside a hard case that needs to be burned by flames before it will break open."

I stop reading aloud, struck by a whole new way of seeing. I regard David's death by fire in an entirely new context, one with a spiritual dimension. I see a way to express my visual and auditory experience of David's suicide straight-on as a poem, using a metaphor as my lens and landscape, as my safe container.

For years, I have needed to write a very direct poem about my sensory experience of my brother's suicide, yet the details are gruesome. How do I speak these terrible images within a redeeming context? My intention is not to shock or to appall—that serves no creative purpose for the reader, nor does it allow much dignity for my brother, whose life has become much bigger than the horror of his death. How to do this?

Out of the blue, I discover a way to unsilence myself. Through the gift of metaphor, through a generative detail about how a eucalyptus seed needs fire to be activated into life. The metaphor of David as a eucalyptus seed has given me both a psychologically safe container and a spiritual landscape for speaking my long-held, sensory truth of bearing witness. It gives me a way to openly claim what I had privately held close for many years. It allows me to make something artistic and spiritually uplifting from hideous memories.

I step into an adjacent room to my desk. While my children play tea party with their stuffed animals, "Gift of Fire" emerges virtually intact, as one pent-up flow of images and words.

Words Make a Way Through Fire

Gift of Fire

"Some eucalyptus seeds develop inside a hard case that needs to be burned by flames before it will break open."
—Trees, Eyewitness Explorer

All along you must have secretly been the seed of
    a eucalyptus.
When I heard you screaming in February air,
and found you, a ball of fire with legs,
I understood you could no longer be my brother.

A few minutes later, you dripped from the yellow bathtub
at the end of the hallway, smoke and the stench of gasoline
wafting like cheap perfume. Tatters of clothing hanging
from your body must have been strips of shell peeling off.
Your bald head the shiny bud underneath.

We cremated your remains.
When Dad and our youngest brother scattered your ashes
years later in the cold waves off the Connecticut coast,
what they really tossed were dusty old roots.

I know now that you completed your cracking,
broke free, claimed new soil, sprouted branches
whose leaves ripple the same currents of air
that flow to my backyard, bring every so often
a gift of fire, faint smell of eucalyptus, fully blooming.

Fire, Gift of Metaphor

◦❦◦

In his book *Free Play*, Stephen Nachmanovitch says,

> I have never ceased to be astounded by the power of writing, music making, drawing or dance to pull me out of sadness, disappointment, depression, bafflement. I am not talking about entertainment or distraction, but of playing, dancing, drawing, writing my way through and out. This process resembles the best in psychotherapy. We don't go away and avoid the troubling thing, but rather confront it in a new framework. The capacity to personify, mythologize, imagine, harmonize is one of the great mercies granted in human life. We are thus able to conceptualize the unknowns of the psyche, to work with forces in us, which, if left unconscious, would overwhelm us. That is the magic of poetry.

Indeed, the magic and the medicine of poetry.

With "Gift of Fire," metaphor gives me a new framework for confronting and reshaping "the troubling thing": horrific memory. Entering into a world of fire as release, and exploring how it might connect to my life, becomes a safe place for remembering. Because this metaphorical world links fire with release, seeding, and starting new life, I can remember a fiery prelude to death without being retraumatized.

While writing "Gift of Fire" does not restore David to healthy life, it allows me another way to integrate the trauma into my larger life. It allows me to birth a more layered and creative way for me to hold memory. It links my experience of bearing witness with regeneration, not just painful extinction.

This reframing of disturbing memory generates an inner shift that I feel with my whole body. It startles in a healing way. It is a physical inner experience. I rise from my desk feeling like I live within a larger sky filled with spring wind. I am changed—more spacious and able to breathe more deeply.

I hold in my heart an ongoing prayer that perhaps David's soul felt released, even as his body was destroyed.

Soon after writing this poem, I begin writing the larger story of David as prose, entitling it "Brother/Sister," writing down as much as I can recall about the days leading up to David's death, as well as childhood memories that feel relevant.

The long process of confronting and reframing my memory continues over years, often with help of a metaphor rooted in the natural world. The Snake River in York, Maine, is an estuary, a transitional world where salt water and fresh water merge. It empties into the Atlantic Ocean, the ocean into which Dad and Peter scattered David's ashes.

My childhood friend Catherine, who along with a handful of steadfast, loving friends, helped see me through high school and the immediate aftermath of David's death, lives now in York. When I visit her in the summer, Catherine takes me swimming in the Snake River. Usually, we jump into the river from Scotland Bridge at high tide near her historic farmhouse, but the first time I experienced the estuary it was by small motorboat, and Catherine took me close to where the mouth of the Snake actually enters the Atlantic.

I jumped off the side of the boat and swam, fascinated by the thickness and taste of the salty water. Water had never felt this way to me before. Eels glided from the grassy banks. The estuary felt both familiar yet strange—inviting yet mysterious.

I thought about David and the blessing of my now peaceful relationship with him. Sometimes I feel David's presence in the daylight world, and sometimes I dream again of a day at the beach with him. On this day, the merged world of estuary resonated with my lived experience that there is a spiritual realm, another kind of merged world where the dead, coming from a

Fire, Gift of Metaphor

limitless ocean, and the living, coming from inland, can communicate in loving ways. I am usually at ease with the reality of "swimming with the dead," in the sense that our lives include relationships with people dead as well as living. This image does not feel haunted to me.

Estuary: The Snake River, Maine

We still find ways to be together.
I am the inland one, still dusting the childhood photos
and stirring the stew

riding the coastal river downstream
until the Snake becomes thick as a tongue
as fresh water merges with salt.

You press inward upon the infinite tide,
more seaweed than flesh.
We meet in a feast of remembrance

my face older than yours now. Still,
you are the elder brother, the one who inhabits
the Huge. When you tell me: *Listen!*

Or your tongue shall make you deaf!
I enter silence as we do the estuary—
plunging off the bow of our small boat.

Jolt of cold. Can't feel or see the bottom.
Shadows ripple beneath us
as eels glide from grassy banks.

We join hands and float on our backs
perfectly content that living
means swimming with the dead—

Words Make a Way Through Fire

The italicized words: "Listen! Or your tongue shall make you deaf!" is a Native American saying that I cherish. This saying speaks to the heart of the practice of poem-making, how it cultivates both a deep inner listening and a quiet, focused attentiveness. We need meditative spaces of creative silence, where we are not talking, where our inward chatter is quiet. Images and feelings then have space to rise from our heart, our imagination, our soul-dreams, and we are open enough to hear and see them, recognize and receive them. Write them down.

Poems serve as a threshold when I write them. Poems offer a way of looking inward and outward simultaneously, rather like Janus, the two-headed Roman god. Poems as threshold provide a safe, sustaining space for taking a deep reflective, listening pause. To linger at the border between the external world and the inward world—a border which accesses both conscious awareness and the revelatory unconscious—can generate such vital insight.

Chapter 9

Extending My Reach

The Children's Bereavement Center of South Texas, 1997

At the Children's Bereavement Center of South Texas
In the room where a long bridge
is painted across a wall,
two girls kneel

beside a white ambulance.
One says, "This father died."
Her sister closes the plastic man
within a tiny coffin,
finds it too big to fit
inside the ambulance,

places it instead on the white roof.
Together they push the toy to the cemetery
beneath the bridge. Unload.

Up the stairs from the kitchen where pictures of the beloved dead are posted, down the hallway from the room where a tree of life shines through the window of the stucco house, I settle in a room with walls painted to evoke the seashore: palm trees, sailboat on the distant horizon, blue waves rolling toward the sandy beach. This will be the writing room for tonight.

The mess of life—love and death—is everywhere. And I feel at home in this mess, this ordered mess I should say, as the making things are contained on shelves—chalk, heart stencils, colored pencils, colored paper, modeling clay, bags of mosaic chips, glue guns, scissors, sharpies, looms, feathers, stickers, stamps, even pipe cleaners.

Finally, I have found a peaceful place within myself and outside myself, here as a writer-in-residence at the Children's Bereavement Center of South Texas (CBC) where I can bring my traumatic grief journey along. Not that my grief journey needs to be the center of my attention anymore, nor of anyone else's attention. It is as much a part of me as my fingertips, earlobes, and kneecaps. I have integrated my traumatic memories, and largely forgiven my sixteen-year-old self for feeling too overwhelmed to offer David love and support the night of his uncontrollable despair. Now, about twenty-four years following David's death, I am ready and eager to offer my attention and support to those who are newly grieving, especially children and young teens struggling to comprehend the suicide of a loved one.

This particular evening is SOS (Survivors of Suicide) group night—the night when children and young people ranging from six years to sixteen who have had a parent recently commit suicide meet at the Children's Bereavement Center (CBC) of South Texas.

Not only do these children deal with loss and grief, but they also struggle with complex feelings of abandonment, betrayal, and confusion. So many questions surround the self-inflicted death of a parent. Why would a person who is guardian of the world for you take his or her own life? Why would your parent not love you enough to want to stay alive? What was so terrible about life or, worse, about you, that wasn't enough? These felt questions whirl through the air.

When Maria enters the writing room, she says to me softly, "I want to write." That is my role, to offer writing as part of a healing process on the nights that offer expressive arts for kids who are survivors of suicide. I offer what I know has worked for me over time.

She tells me that she is in fourth grade. What I already know is that Maria lives with her aunt (her mother's sister) and an older cousin. Her aunt meets with the adult group downstairs, and her cousin is in the attic room with the older kids. Her brothers and sisters live with another aunt. I don't know how often she sees them. For nearly a year, she has lived this arrangement, ever since her mother took her own life. Her father had died in a car accident several years before her mother's suicide.

The small table is already full of younger children, and Maria likes the idea of working on the carpeted floor. She knows what she wants: to write and to work with clay on the floor. I locate a tablet of construction paper from the closet. Maria selects a sheet of white. Clay is needed, so I return to the closet and find a new package of modeling clay that we open together.

She begins with blue, layering it at the bottom of the vertical page. "What do you think this is?" she asks me.

I consider for a moment and say, "It makes me think of the ocean."

She smiles. "This is going to be the beach."

"Are you making a picture of a memory that you have?"

She nods.

Waiting to see how writing might eventually fit into her process, I involve myself in my own activity beside her on the floor. My supplies are a sheet of yellow paper and thin-tipped markers. I begin with the words "broken pot"; I don't write them straightforwardly. Instead, I draw inspiration from the poet

Words Make a Way Through Fire

E. E. Cummings and create an image by carefully misplacing my letters. Inside the *b* I tuck a small *r*. The segments of the letters *k* and *n* disconnect. I write a large *P* and place an *O* inside of the round space with a tiny *t* inside of that.

I vary my colors: begin with purple, move to brown and silver, back to purple, then orange.

"My sand is all different colors." Maria's voice draws my attention back to her page. Above the blue clay she has layered white, silver, pale yellow, and taupe.

I say, "The sand on the beach looks like different colors depending upon the light."

Maria nods and returns to her work. "My mom was always saying that she would take me to the beach, and she never did."

I realize that the scene unfolding beside me does not arise from memory. Rather, it represents deep desire for what can never be: It creates a moment that this child will never share with her mother at the beach. What was promised and then what was taken from her forever. Maria understands instinctively through her making hands and eyes that she can give herself her heart's deep yearning. She looks into the abyss of her loss and imagines a colorful scene. Through a creative process, she can manifest an unlived day at the beach with her mother.

Next on the page appears a large, bright red umbrella attached to a long pole. Beneath the red umbrella stands the slender yellow body of her mother. She receives long brown hair that hints of streaming in the beach breeze. And she wears bright red lipstick because, as Maria tells me, red is her mother's favorite color of lipstick. Beside her emerges a smaller yellow figure with pink lipstick and shorter brown hair secured with red barrettes.

"You have the same color hair as your mother," I say. "You have your mother's hair."

"But mine is in pigtails."

Extending My Reach

    This girl beside me works so steadily, without hesitation. At one point, Maria interrupts her work to notice what emerges on my yellow page. She puzzles out the odd arrangement of letters to read "broken pot" and mentions the clay gardening pot that had been broken earlier in the evening while all the children were gathered at once—deliberately broken by a facilitator, and the pieces distributed among us.

    I continue writing while Maria returns to her red clay. I write straightforwardly, "When my brother died, soon after he died, my sad and mad heart felt like a broken pot." Then I write two questions: "Where have all my pieces gone? Where did he go?" I write them in such a way that they share the word "where." Above all these words, I write, "Who am I now?" It's written upside down.

    One of the other children finishes his clay creation and talks with another facilitator. He speaks his mother's name, she is dead by suicide, too, and the facilitator writes it on the inside of a broken pot shard. "Anna," he repeats loudly.

    Maria looks up, startled. "Anna? That is my mother's name." She regards her creation. It is vivid, detailed, and seems to deeply satisfy Maria. A quiet glow radiates around her as she beholds what her hands have made, what her eyes are seeing, defining, restoring to her being.

    I feel the center in this child, and I feel the child hearing her own center speak. At this point the speaking consists of wordless, powerful images. I am witnessing this child transform grief and hurt into color and line. Maria is beginning to define what her life signifies to her. She is claiming her soul. The symbolic processes of art along with her yearning imagination are integral tools for this transformation. Perhaps the way has been cleared for words.

    "Are you ready to tell the story of your picture now?"

    "Now that I am finished, I am ready."

Words Make a Way Through Fire

"Would you like to write it down, or would you like me to write it down?"

"You write it down."

Maria tells me what to write. It is largely a description of what she has shaped, a kind of naming that includes the color of mother and daughter's hair, the red barrettes. But she also adds details that cannot be seen in the picture. In the hidden world of her picture the ocean is safe, free of fish and sharks. Only porpoises are allowed in this water. As Maria comes to the end of her telling, she finally hesitates, fumbling for a word as she seeks to name the emotional tone of her day with her mother at the beach.

"It's like *fubulous* and it means fun and silly."

"Do you mean *frivolous*?"

"Yes, frivolous!" Maria is pleased that her meaning has been recognized. I place it at the end of her story about her imaginary day at the beach with her mother. She writes her name and places today's date. She asks, "My mother's name is—should I use *was* instead of *is*?"

"You may use *is* if you wish."

"My mother's name is Anna."

While the yellow page filled with her words is light and easy to carry, the white page layered with clay is heavy, harder to manage. It needs a sturdy backing. We find a thick piece of cardboard and cut it slowly to a smaller size. As Maria glues the two pages to the cardboard, we hear voices below singing in the closing circle. The evening has drawn to a close as Maria has drawn her heart's desire on the page in clay and carefully chosen words. She takes her creation down the winding stairs to the living room of the bereavement house. I stay upstairs briefly to put away the scissors and ragged remnant of cardboard.

Later, I learn from another facilitator that as Maria showed her cousin and aunt what she had made, her cousin rearranged

Extending My Reach

lines of her clay, as if he knew best how to place such materials. His mother, Maria's aunt, looked on without protecting the creation from the boy's disrespectful hands. The observer saw Maria's eyes turn blank, then fill with sadness. She was left alone and defenseless amid such interference. When I hear this, I remember the peaceful feel of Maria's working, how that making time radiated with the soft flare that accompanies the unfolding of inward healing. I ache for her loneliness and for the shocking loss at such a young age of her mother, both her parents.

Then, I realize that no one and nothing in time can ever take this fresh making time away from her; it lives within her now regardless of how a resentful and perhaps confused cousin might tamper with the outcome of her creation—I feel some comfort. Strength lives in Maria, an inner knowing of how to give herself some of what she needs, a memory of a "frivolous" day at the beach that never took place, yet which becomes real as memory through the symbolic power of deliberately shaped, colorful clay. And through lines of words on yellow paper. I marvel at her instinctive reaching toward art for solace, for breathing room and expression of an innermost self that seeks healing through artful play. What kind of tenacity will this child have as she struggles to name her own experience as the daughter of a mother who committed suicide?

I am grateful that a center focused on the therapeutic arts exists to help families find their way through loss, whether that loss occurred by natural means, accident, or as the outcome of violence. Having a bereavement community to support my parents, my brothers, and myself following David's suicide would have been a great comfort. Survivors of suicide can feel so terribly alone, and blameworthy.

Working at the CBC allows me a broader lens through which I can regard my experience of being a survivor of suicide;

the nature of my questions and concerns shifts. Now that I have forgiven myself and no longer feel haunted, I can consider David's suicide from his perspective. I can reflect on his undiagnosed yet vividly apparent depression—its responsibility for David's desolation, and thus, for his suicide.

David had an unusual capacity for compassion; he cared deeply about other people. How could he have chosen violence? How could he have harmed himself so severely, inflicting such suffering on himself and devastating his family?

I am sharing a glass of wine with a dear friend, and speaking my questions when she turns quiet, which is significant for such an animated, articulate woman. She looks inward, takes a deep breath, and says that she once suffered from persistent depression. "It was as if someone else was taking me over slowly. A little bit more each day, each week."

This image lingers in my imagination and in my heart. For the next few days, I cannot stop thinking about it. While I understood intellectually that severe depression can distort a person's view of self and reality, I had not allowed myself to imagine what it would feel like to be inhabited by depression. What would that feel like inside your whole being?

In a sense, relentless depression is an invisible and internal disease, a disease of the mind and heart rather than of the body. And, yet it must come to feel like an entire landscape, a world or even a kind of body within which you live and move, think and imagine, feel.

It affects people in highly individual ways, and doesn't always result in suicide, although most people who commit suicide are depressed. It transforms the highly personal inner world of perception, making it difficult for family members to know how thoroughly depression has taken root. Clinical depression can lead people to commit desperate, violent acts that are otherwise out of character.

Extending My Reach

How does anyone make sense out of the dynamic between depression as a disease and the person who harbors the disease? Who is really making the choice to commit suicide: the depression or the person being inhabited by depression? What kind of schism within the self is created by relentless depression?

Chapter 10

Piecing David's Life Together

Having pieced myself largely back together, I feel compelled to piece together my understanding of David's life, from my limited point of view. Having processed my trauma to the degree that I no longer instantly recall him aflame or wrapped in bandages, I experience earlier memories with my brother. Fragments surface. I find myself wondering: What do I know about my brother's life? What is knowable? Might weaving what is knowable into a new perspective help gentle all that I don't know, give me a solid human being to hold onto and to honor in memory?

One of my earliest, clearest memories is of David weeping. I am watching from the stairs as Mother takes David by the hand, leads him into Dad's small study, and closes the door. Some minutes later, they emerge. My brother's nine-year-old face is wet with tears. I don't understand why David has cried.

Now I know that Mother gave him the news that Ta, our grandmother, had died. Unlike me, David was old enough to know this grandmother, old enough to grieve her death. Weeks before Ta's death, David wrote her a letter that Mother had mailed, then gathered from among Ta's things, and kept.

Piecing David's Life Together

Dear Ta,
 How are you feeling? I hope you will have a happy Easter. I am sad and glad that I am going to Cincinnati. I'm glad because I will live closer to you, and I am sad because I will leave Aunt Jane and my friends.
 Your loving grandson, David

A few months after David writes that letter, and a few months following Ta's death from colorectal cancer diagnosed too late for effective treatment, we move from Old Greenwich, Connecticut, far inland to Cincinnati, Ohio. We leave the ocean and extended family—cousins who feel like friends, Mother's sister Jane, and our paternal grandparents in New York City. It's an unfortunate turning point. I feel these losses immediately, especially the absence of the ocean and its soothing, playful influence upon my family.

Gone is the rhythmic sound of the ocean, the tug and tumble of waves, sand sliding away from my feet. Gone are sensations of popping bubbles of seaweed, scrambling away from jellyfish floating near shore, dashing barefoot across the blazing August sand, eating ice cream sandwiches that melt quickly. There is no more lying outstretched on the beach following lunch of peanut butter and jelly sandwiches, listening to Mother with her myriad of dramatic voices read *Peter Pan* and *Mary Poppins*. Gone are magical evenings of roasting hot dogs around a campfire near the trees as migrating monarchs flicker in bright orange waves. Gone are Dad's endearing stories about being a Baby Pirate who sails great oceans in his bathtub boat called the *Knife and Fork*, accompanied by a parrot named Lulu Belle and a whale named Stanley—stories infused by the distant voice of the listening ocean.

In Cincinnati, Dad disappears into a new job. No longer do we pick him up at the train station; he drives himself to

Words Make a Way Through Fire

work. Dad stops telling us stories, something that brought us together. Once we move inland, not only does the ocean vanish, but also the imaginative stories that took place upon the ocean. Most regretful of all, the storyteller vanishes along with the stories, becomes preoccupied by work.

My childlike sense of being held within a family circle dissolves. An inarticulate feeling of dislocation, loss, and isolation drifts through the house on Compton Road.

For one school year, we live in a rental house. It has an in-ground, backyard pool that serves as poor replacement for the rocky coastline where I learned to swim. Our front yard is an extension of the sharp bend of Compton Road: a kind of elbow jutting outward. Mother says, "If a driver ever takes the bend too fast, he'll end up in our living room. It happened once to the next-door neighbors."

Across the hall from my room is my parents' room. Down the hall, Noel and Peter share a room. David, now almost ten, has a small room near the downstairs porch. Sleeping downstairs alone and on the same level as the backyard pool bothers him. He mentions recurring dreams about shrinking and being swallowed up by the pool. He spends a lot of time in the basement training his parakeet to sit on his shoulder while he plucks "When the Saints Go Marching In" on his ukulele.

Mother doesn't unpack fully. She doesn't want this move to Cincinnati. Just when she needs most the emotional support of her sister Jane as they grieve Ta's death, Mother is uprooted to a city where she has neither family nor friends.

In the kitchen with the Dutch doors, where the bottom half could be locked while the top door stood wide open, Mother expresses her unhappiness and grief as frustration and rage. She flings pots and pans across the linoleum, denting the metal pots. When Mother is making a meal, we stay out of the kitchen and out of her way.

Piecing David's Life Together

As a six-year-old, I have not seen this side of my mother before. Who has she become? What has changed her? Her anger finds another more disturbing expression as the year progresses.

I can only imagine what this uneasy transition feels like for David with his more mature, ten-year-old awareness. One day, a most distressing childhood incident takes place. A neighbor friend named Phoebe gives me a piggy bank that she made from clay. It is shaped like an elephant and painted gray and pink. This thoughtful, handmade gift from a new friend feels like a treasure to me. I place the bank on a table while searching for coins. As I return clutching a few quarters, David shoves the elephant deliberately onto the floor as he walks by. The bank breaks into many pieces. Outraged, I tell Mother what he has done. When she questions him, he smart-mouths her. She erupts. She grabs one of Dad's belts and lunges toward David, who then runs out the front door and along the edge of Compton Road. Mother chases him, swatting the belt at the back of his pumping legs again and again, until she catches him. She swats him on his bottom and marches him home to apologize.

"I'm sorry for breaking your bank," he says, red-faced and teary-eyed. Mother stands by, her mouth closed and taut, gripping Dad's belt.

Alarmed by the violence that Mother has just inflicted on my brother, and feeling strangely responsible for it, I don't know what to say to David. Never have I seen my mother react so fiercely. Never have I seen her strike one of my brothers.

"That's alright," I mumble.

"Well, if it's alright, then why did I get in such trouble," David sputters and strides away. Confused and scared by what had happened, I pick up a shard of the elephant trunk and retreat to my secret space.

My secret space is a small cupboard built inside my bedroom wall. In the middle of the wall is a small square door, about eye level to my six-year-old self. The handle is round, white and stamped with a red rose. When I pull the door open, daylight falls on the snug, dark world within. I stand on a small chair and climb into the wall—just enough room for me to sit inside with a few treasures. This small, self-contained space becomes my refuge from Mother's rages. The only person with whom I share it is Phoebe, who knows about matches. Phoebe teaches me how to strike matches and burn candles held by a silver-plated candlestick. I light the dark enclosure, secretly burning candles inside the wall of my room with the doors closed.

Hidden away, I feel safe. The small flame pushes back the darkness. There is just enough flickering light to read by, or to play with my stuffed red doll. I can almost hear distant ocean waves. I can almost hear stories in my father's voice. Stranded in landlocked Ohio, with a mother who has become volatile and unfamiliar, and an absent father, I half expect a stranger's car will crash through our living room. At least I have my secret campfire, my private space with its musty air and shadows winging all around me while the flame slowly burns the candle down.

We live in the rental house for only one year, during which Mother takes after David with Dad's belt repeatedly when she feels provoked by him. During the summer, we move to another part of Cincinnati called Indian Hill where the school system is highly regarded, and each house has a large yard. Some of the most well-heeled families in Cincinnati reside in Indian Hill, some with grand mansions, sprawling grounds with fountains, tennis courts, and large fields for their horses. The nondescript, ranch-style house our parents buy is situated on the corner of DeMar Road and Rettig Lane: a private lane of long, well-tended lawns that culminates in a dead end, behind which wind acres of green belt.

Piecing David's Life Together

Throughout my childhood and adolescence, I find the house lonely, unlit, and divisive. The narrow hallways, small rooms, and small windows feel confining and isolating. Along one side of the house are four bedrooms: mine on the corner with the tiny bathroom, then the small rooms for David, Peter, and Noel, connected by a windowless hallway that ends at a shared bathroom. On the other side of the house is our parents' room, and Dad's dark study. Dad's study smells of hundreds of undusted, hardback books that spill from the floor-to-ceiling bookshelves. In between the two wings is a narrow kitchen that overlooks a side yard, and a dining room and living area that has tall windows darkened by heavy, ancient, embroidered drapes that once belonged to Ta.

While Mother's fits of unleashed fury diminish and Dad becomes more involved at home, I never regain my sense of emotional security within the family. My eyes are opened to my mother's volatility and to my father's remove. Part of me continues to climb metaphorically into a secret space, when I sense a situation becoming electric and chaotic.

I spend as much time as possible outdoors. Our backyard is a flat expanse made for a softball game or for Frisbee throwing, one of David's delights. Sometimes we manage to trim the grass that grows under the rickety wooden fence paralleling the lane. A cluster of tall and full-hipped pine trees just outside the living room is perfect for chasing our Labrador named Jason, a game invented by David. Jason learns to chase motorcycles that travel sometimes along DeMar Road, and eventually we give him to a Kentucky farmer.

After Jason leaves our family, David develops a relationship with a young hunting dog who lives a few streets away. The father in the household keeps the dog caged, away from the play of even his children, because he wants strictly a hunting companion. David ignores all instructions to leave the dog alone.

Words Make a Way Through Fire

He releases the dog from her pen and chases her around the yard. When the determined neighbor places a padlock on the door, David climbs the high walls and drops down into the pen where they play until both end up snuggling side by side in confinement.

At the end of Rettig Lane stretches acres of woods with a mostly dry creek. We safely wander those woods for hours, looking for fossils. After heavy rain, we splash in a deep section of the creek bed filled with several feet of water. More often, we congregate with the other children on someone's long lawn and play Ghost in the Graveyard, Capture the Flag, Red Rover, and soccer, even in snow.

But David rarely joins in these neighborhood games. When with us siblings, he exuberantly launches a Frisbee across the yard in a rousing game of Pickle. Gradually, he tends more and more toward being solitary.

As a young teen, David is quick to absorb information relating to electronics. Mac, his one close friend, remembers a time early in their friendship when David constructed a tiny amplifier from various transistor parts scattered about the room.

"We were probably thirteen. I wanted to take my electric guitar to California for my near deaf grandmother. She was a musician. David rigged up a little earphone to the thing, and it actually worked."

Soon afterward, David begins studying electronics with a graduate student, assisting him with a project in the neonatal intensive care unit of the university hospital, developing new monitors and identifying old monitors that need to be grounded anew. He loves being part of that project with its purpose of helping newborns survive their premature birth.

By the time David enters high school he is stocky and uncommonly strong and looks everyone straight in the eye through black glasses with thick lenses. He has a distinctive way of moving that is rambling yet graceful. For a while, he is a wrestler. In our living room, he shows me shoulder rolls learned during wrestling. He removes his glasses, takes a running step or two, throws his compact body into a quick roll across his right shoulder, then springs into position, ready to repeat the roll back across the carpet. Over and over David shows me this move, like a dancer practicing his steps. The last time I see him make this series of moves, he is aflame, and responding to my desperate cry to "Roll!"

The day comes when David's wrestling coach urges him to hold his opponent long enough to inflict pain. David refuses and quits the wrestling team. I think he knew all too well what it is like to be physically hurt by someone powerful, or who at least has the situational advantage. From time to time, when Dad is not at home, Mother still strikes out angrily and briefly at her muscular, nearly full-grown son. He begins defending himself and strikes back. I never see him initiate the physical contact with Mom. Following some bruised ribs, Mother stops hitting David.

In 1970, when he turns sixteen, David becomes increasingly rebellious and restless. Indian Hill High School bores him. He grows his stringy hair long, takes up smoking cigarettes and marijuana, and plays his rock music loud. From a family friend, David purchases a ten-year-old white Mercedes sedan with red leather interior and headlights that he describes as cross-eyed. It also has amazing suspension. Once, I have the dubious honor of riding between the front seats as David drives a carload of siblings and friends over the small hills and tight bends of Cunningham Road in Indian Hill. He is a skillful if not always restrained driver. The roads are dry that day, and I emerge far less bounced and bruised than I will a few years later as a seat-belted passenger in the back seat of a friend's small American car that careens off the very same road, slick with rain, and wraps itself around a telephone pole.

Words Make a Way Through Fire

For a few summer months in 1971, David and his friend Geof head west in the Mercedes, eager to see the country and to experience the vibes of a nation still struggling with civil unrest relating to the Vietnam War and civil rights. The Mercedes has mechanical problems, which become expensive, and leaves them at the mercy of small-town mechanics able to fix an older car. With their long hair, David and Geof must seem like hippies to the small-town folks they meet along the way. They mention going to a peace march near Berkeley where FBI agents "stepped out of a car with government plates, wearing their inconspicuous trench coats, sporting a bulge where their guns were, and dark glasses to make them invisible."

They return to DeMar at around 2:00 a.m. from their adventure, with two hitchhikers in tow. Noel and I rouse, make them bacon and scrambled eggs. Mother and Dad eventually waken to the commotion and cigarette smoke, enter the kitchen, glad to see their eldest son home safely. David says suddenly, "I am so incredibly burned out. I was tailgating a semi with my foot off the gas, just floating along from the suction, and using his lights in all that fog tonight." He shakes his head in disbelief.

His Mercedes doesn't last many months past that great American West adventure. David does what he can to keep the Mercedes functioning. Eventually, he parks the broken-down car as discreetly as possible in our large yard, behind some evergreen bushes.

David often extends himself to others in need. While driving through Kentucky, heading for the suspension bridge that leads across the Ohio River and into Cincinnati toward home, he notices a family stranded by the side of the road. Their car has broken down. David's mechanical skills can't make the needed difference, so he gives the father a ride to a public telephone and back. With his last few dollars, he buys milk for the children.

Piecing David's Life Together

Another time, when he is driving our family's Volkswagen van around Cincinnati, David picks up a hitchhiker bound for Tennessee. My brother decides to deliver the surprised hiker to his destination. The round-trip journey takes several days. We don't know where he is until he returns home with a sheepish smile, an explanation, and metric tools missing out of the van. He has run out of money and traded the tools for a tankful of gas.

David nearly flunks out of our college preparatory high school, yet he is so well-read that he can discuss all the books on the sophomore English reading list that first week of school. He lacks discipline, yet when really hooked on something, he pours himself into it. I watch him draw and color a giant map of Africa, attending to it quietly night after night, stretched out on the linoleum floor of our kitchen. The map is beautiful—meticulously sketched on heavy cardboard, each country given a different color and its name inscribed with careful handwriting. The colors he chooses are soft, well-balanced as they define country after country across the large expanse of a continent still gripped by apartheid.

David can't quite organize his talents into a purposeful plan of action. He finally quits attending public school and enrolls in an alternative high school. He writes me a letter in August of 1971, when I am away at summer camp.

Mon., 16 Aug '71
Dear Cy,
  Mac and I just returned from a canoe trip as did Dad and Pete; Noel is back from Hocking Valley; my room still needs cleaning; my car, so far, has been neglected, so I'll be working like the dickens on it for the rest of the week. Revelation of the hour: Some people are nice, and some aren't. Are you having a contest at your camp to see who gets the most letters? Coke machines are fun.

Words Make a Way Through Fire

If yours has bottles stacked horizontally, you can open the bottles with a bottle opener and put a cup (a big one) underneath to catch the Coke (I prefer Dr. Pepper). If they're stacked vertically, you can open them with a bottle opener and suck out the contents with a straw.

It isn't luck that I am going to New Morning—I planned it. I really wish that at least you and Noel would accompany me. I am <u>soundly convinced</u> that Indian Hill isn't the place for any of us and that New Morning is. Indian Hill is a super fuck-up. You have more than a fair opportunity to do what you want to do and get a good <u>education</u>—not schooling—at New Morning. I know, <u>very well</u>, how you would feel about leaving Indian Hill because you would miss your friends and some teachers. But just think what it would be like to do what was important to you, what you like, during the school year. You can go anywhere and do anything you want to do, anytime and not get fucked at every turn by things people <u>require</u> of you, and which aren't relevant to you.

If it weren't for New Morning, I'd be going to Indian Hill this year, but instead I have an <u>alternative</u>—New Morning—and I'm taking <u>initiative</u>—making my own decision—and going there during my last school year.

Much love,
Dave
P.S. I have a summer cold—when is fall?

New Morning does not serve David well; it is too unstructured. He never graduates from high school. A turning point is needed, a sense of purpose and belief in self.

At the very end of 1972, when he turns eighteen, David moves temporarily to New York City. He is keen to make some

Piecing David's Life Together

money delivering packages for the United Parcel Service and to keep our grandfather company. Our father's father, whom we called Granpappy, has been deeply lonely following the unexpected death of his wife, our grandmother. Oma died a few years earlier on an understaffed, post-surgical unit while frantically calling for nursing help that was unresponsive.

While David waits for a job to become available, he and Granpappy dispute the acceptability of long hair on a young man. It is easy to imagine that, as a former judge born during the Victorian era and one who served on a prestigious, international court of restitution in Berlin, Granpappy assumes a disdainful air.

David abruptly packs his things and storms out of the four-story row house on Garden Place. He has no car, little money, and it is winter. A few days later, someone from the United Parcel Service calls asking to interview David, who has since disappeared.

For weeks, we have no idea where David is or when we will see him again. He finally sends one postcard to let us know that he is alive. "I have nothing on my mind," he writes and signs the message with the symbol for pi. We assume he is hitchhiking his way across the country, making up his journey as he moves along.

It is nearly spring when Dad receives a phone call from a psychiatrist in Seattle, asking if he wants to talk with David. "Oh God, yes!"

When David gets on the phone he asks, "Do you want me back?"

"Yes, I do! Yes, we do! As soon as possible. We have been so very worried about you," Dad replies, then he and David cry together on the phone. David flies home a few days later.

When Dad brings David home from the airport, thirteen-year-old Peter walks first through the back door to the driveway to greet him. David sobs and enfolds our young brother into his arms, holding onto him for a long, long time, desperate for comfort.

What actually took place for David during those long months of wandering alone is never clear. The Seattle psychiatrist doesn't give my parents many details about David's brief stay in his unit.

David had been staying in Salvation Army shelters along the West Coast. It was policy in those days that guests were expected to leave following three consecutive nights in the shelter. David had spent his three allotted nights in the Seattle shelter and faced the lonely decision of where to go next. Some older man had been lurking about and bothering David in a manner mentioned yet left unexplained. It's easy to imagine that David couldn't take it anymore—a sense of failure, frustration, alienation, and homelessness gnawing within him.

There, in the Salvation Army shelter in a city far from home, a city known for its rain, a city that our mother will choose to move to nearly twenty years later, I now imagine that David stands beside a battered cot, his few rumpled clothes stuffed in a backpack, his long hair unwashed, and his leather boots heavy on his feet, and he starts to cry. As other homeless individuals look on in astonishment, his deep sobs turn into wails, and then screams. Not knowing that this lost soul with the powerful biceps is far too gentle to turn violent, the shelter officials call for help. David probably resists and is placed in a straitjacket, then admitted to a psychiatric unit for a few days. Once contact is made with our family, he returns home.

David of the generous, restless spirit is never quite the same person following this final cross-country journey. From time to time he grabs onto Dad and simply wails. Peter becomes aware of David disappearing frequently into the bathroom, turning on the fan, and smoking marijuana or hashish. I notice him

Piecing David's Life Together

sitting often at his desk in his room next to mine, feet propped up, smoking unfiltered Pall Malls and staring wordlessly into vacant air as if in a trance.

One night, I wake up to find him sitting beside my bed with his flashlight, slowly pulling the sheets from my legs. "What are you doing?" I ask him.

"I'm crazy."

"No, you're not. You're just acting crazy. Now go back to bed." He leaves obediently with his flashlight.

A few weeks later, as I stand in my small shower rinsing shampoo from my hair, David opens the door and steps naked into the stall. He does so in such a perfectly natural way that I am more astonished than alarmed. There is a childlike innocence in my brother's demeanor; he doesn't seem entirely present, as if he is really stoned. I show him what to do—take the soap and run it along his arms, and then rinse. Then I turn off the water, quietly direct him to open the door, and tell him where he can find a towel. He stands, unsure of what to do next. I direct him to go to his room and get dressed in clean clothes. He does, and we never speak of it again. Neither does he venture into my room again.

I tell our parents about this incident. Dad installs a lock on my door and gets a referral for a family therapist.

Mother says that the few psychiatrists with whom they consulted over the years, beginning when David was in middle school, fell short of using the word "schizophrenia." Dad recalls that one psychiatrist characterized David as "a lightning rod." David lives intensely, loving and suffering keenly. How much of his intensity reflects a natural passion for life that never found its fullest creative expression, how much of that intensity reflects a chemical imbalance within his brain, and how much of his inward suffering reverberates with Mother's inconsistently inflicted, yet recurring pattern of aggression will never be clear.

Words Make a Way Through Fire

1974, the year of David's death, is the tail end of the Vietnam War era. A disturbing photograph of Buddhist monk Thich Quang Duc sitting serenely in the lotus position on a street in Saigon engulfed in self-inflicted flames is widely shown in newspapers and magazines. Taken in 1963, it is linked with protest and sacrifice, and becomes part of the visual documentation of that unpopular war. Thich Quang Duc leaves behind a statement lamenting the immorality of war.

I learn the word "self-immolation" as I read a caption for the photo published in *Life* magazine. It is an image both shocking and strangely fascinating. How could a living, burning man remain so still inside a thicket of smoke and flames?

On some level, David has a relationship with fire that includes creativity, bringing pieces together. He learns welding. He gives Mac a small abstract sculpture that he has made, welding pieces of rusty metal with a black glue and carefully administered fire. Some part of David's mind understands the properties of controlled fire.

One evening after his return from Seattle, David drives to Clifton, where the University of Cincinnati is situated near downtown Cincinnati, and he doesn't return. Dad finally locates him at the Work House, a detention center where David had been taken following an angry response to a police officer pushing him against a restaurant wall, thinking David was someone else. During detention, David sets his mattress alight, causing alarm. In this situation, fire may have served as a way of getting attention, as well as a form of protest.

On the heels of David's return from Seattle, another dismaying turn of events shapes our family. Following a series of debilitating strokes, Granpappy is moved from the row house in Brooklyn Place to live in my room, while I sleep in the detached family room. During the few months that Granpappy lives in my room with its small but private bathroom, we witness gradual mental erosion become senility. Our proper grandfather with the brilliant legal mind, the pipe-smelling patrician who wears three-piece suits with a gold watch whether he is playing chess with Noel, showing us his collection of ancient Roman coins, or sipping a martini, is transformed stroke by small stroke into an isolated, deeply depressed man.

Not long before he moves into a nearby town house where he has constant care, I sit with our grandfather at our dining room table to keep him company while Mother prepares his lunch of tomato soup and a cheese sandwich. Wearing a silk paisley dressing gown, he sits quietly at the head of the table where my father usually sits. With his knife and fork, he begins cutting an invisible slice of meat on the thick cloth placemat. He then lifts the fork to his mouth and chews. Surely, he will notice the empty taste of air, I think. My grandfather does not. When Mother places the real bowl of soup before him, he is distressed and bewildered. He is certain that he has already eaten. I don't know how to process this strange behavior from such an intellectual, accomplished man.

When Granpappy relocates, I am grateful to have my own room back, and relieved to no longer witness my proper grandfather act undignified because of his mental confusion. We visit him as a family perhaps once or twice. When it becomes clear that Granpappy soon will die, Dad asks us if we want to visit him a last time. Neither Noel, Peter, nor I agree to go, preferring to keep our distance. David, despite having reason to hold a grudge against the man whose critical words drove him alone into winter, calls on Granpappy. David is the only grandchild with compassion enough to pay final respects to our last remaining grandparent. I love and admire my brother's grace in this moment.

Granpappy dies at his town house attended by Mother who keeps vigil through his final breath, while Dad is out of town.

Words Make a Way Through Fire

Finally, our grandfather is at peace. He is cremated late in 1973, a few weeks before my sixteenth birthday on December 12.

David drives me to take the test for my driver's permit. When we arrive at the testing site, I realize that I have forgotten my birth certificate. With great patience, David drives me home to retrieve it, then returns me for the driving test. He lets me drive home with my new license. Two months later, my nineteen-year-old brother is cremated as well.

Indigo

From the clutch of Mother's memorabilia found
after her death, this photograph is new to me—

my oldest brother as a nine-year-old with slick, cropped hair
cupping a parakeet inside his already broad hands:

such tenderness in his eyes as he bows his head
slightly over the bird. He looks smitten

as our mother holding him as a newborn,
her firstborn, standing at the window of the Army

hospital the day following his birth, tilting
David toward the viewer, presumably our father.

His infant eyes and round mouth open as if receiving
the morning sunlight as first communion. Much is

beginning in these photographs, and memory
now tilts its wounded way through me—

suddenly I am standing in the basement
of our rental house on Compton Road

Piecing David's Life Together

where David releases the parakeet from its cage.
He invites me to bring my index finger alongside his,

let the bird step from his finger to mine.
As I do, the clutch of clawed feet startles me.

Stroke his wing feathers, David says, *feel how soft*.
Indigo! The bird was named for a color but not

this bird's color which is a blue turquoise.
Indigo, the color of devotion—David training

the bird to land upon his shoulder and stay there
while he builds another fort with his wooden blocks,

Indigo ruffling wings and cocking his small head when
David forgets to move gently, mindful of the feathered

weight he carries.

Part Two

Voice

And I walked naked
from the beginning
breathing in
my life,
breathing out
poems.
—Excerpt from "A Cloak" by Denise Levertov

Levitation

The path emerges as you go:

> when some bright impulse
> urges you forward from solid

ground upon the open air—
(I say *upon* rather than *into*

> because when stepping
> you do not plunge

into cactus rumpling the canyon floor)
something does hold: an invisible stone,

> tangle of spider web
> or July heat solidifying.

Trust your lightness the quiet says:
you have been plummeting for years

> *and letting me catch you*
> *with net of wind and web.*

Your bones are made from clouds,
they know how to levitate.

> See that campfire
> on the facing ridge—

keep walking toward those beckoning flames.

Chapter 11

Haiku Healing

South Texas Brush Country, March 2020

In January 2020, an unfamiliar spaciousness unfolds before me. For the first time in eighteen years, I am not teaching writing and literature courses at St. Mary's University in San Antonio. During the previous October, I had surprised myself by declining my chairwoman's offer of a spring schedule. I love teaching, and I love my students. Yet, I feel strongly that I am not supposed to teach in the spring, for reasons that are unclear. I know to trust my intuition. Perhaps Voice is sending me a message that would clarify eventually.

Soon after New Year's Day, it begins as a felt sound, like a distantly rumbling train that has been trying to unload its passengers for decades but can't quite find the right platform in the thick fog of night.

An image surfaces: returning to what I had started twenty-seven years ago as "Brother/Sister." Something within me feels ready: ready to gather and edit prose pieces that already exist, ready to imagine what else wants to enter the story. Certain poems written over the course of twenty-seven years now belong to the narrative weave. What feels at the center of the story now is how the meaning of traumatic memory can be dynamic, transformational, and threaded with beautiful moments when the wounded heart, jolted mind, and watchful soul find voice through poetry and feel held by the sacred. A new title comes to mind: "My Brother's Cup."

I know that to answer this call, I will need a measure of fairly uninterrupted time and quiet space. As I draft a proposal for one writing residency, I am offered an entirely different writing residency that I didn't know existed—a month to write in solitude on a privately owned, working ranch, courtesy of the San Ysidro Ranch Writing Residency.

The Restless Story and Trying Once Again to Finish It

In my dream, the train calls out through the long dark, preparing to arrive, unload its passengers. But it falls short of the platform which hovers vaguely in the fog. No one can disembark, so it reverses along the tracks already traveled to try approaching once more. There is much sleeplessness. Those who wait to greet their loved ones have waited years for a reunion always on the verge of occurring—they hunger for embrace, imagine the face of a dearly departed, never quite returned. On the platform, they lean into the dark when they hear the whistle, feel the tracks begin to rumble. Surely, this time! And what about those on board? They have gathered their threadbare belongings, their crumpled papers and paperback books so handled that pages have fallen out and covers are torn. They have memorized the opening thirty pages. They are not yet beyond hunger but memory of fullness fades. The train itself is tireless. The locomotive has rusted, but the momentum of a journey keeps the fire roaring.

On the first day of March, I leave our green hill aglow with fragrant mountain laurels and blooming redbud trees, and I drive southwest toward South Texas brush country. The closer I get to the San Ysidro Ranch, the more the land flattens and relinquishes color. Although I have been told by the owner of the ranch, who sponsors the residency, to expect a drought-stricken landscape, I am not prepared for how austere the land appears. When I enter the gates, I am taken aback by the expanse of scrubby gray branches. None of the mesquite trees are budding. Hardly a shred of green brightens the expanse. Off the main ranch road, Istana Cabin, where I will reside for a month, is encircled by a gravel drive and a dozen bare-branched mesquite trees. The yard is primarily dirt, with few patches of sparse grass and prairie verbena. Beyond extends a long, colorless horizon.

With the flourishing of spring fresh in my mind, I am disheartened by the prospect of dwelling within this barren region for a month. I remind myself to be open to where I am, choose to be receptive. I tell myself to stop judging the landscape for what it is not and learn to see its beauty. The sunset my first night is stunning. From my seated perspective on the porch, the setting sun pauses at the heart of a mesquite tree, lights a brief fire, then slips below the horizon. My spirit lifts.

The next morning, I realize that the cabin is oriented east-west to take advantage of the north-south breezes. I can step outside on the porch facing east and watch the sunrise. At end of day, I can step outside to the porch facing west and watch the sunset. The cabin is a sundial!

The air is utterly still that first afternoon, humid and breathless. Not a single bare branch moves. I feel discouraged again by this suffocating environment. Then comes a monarch butterfly flickering through the barren trees! What joy, what visual relief flows from this flurry of color amid stillness.

I resolve that I will begin each day at Istana Cabin by writing a haiku; surely this mindfulness practice will help attune me to the landscape's minimalist beauty. I want to notice any gradual evidence of spring and appreciate simple things such as an orange butterfly flickering through a leafless tree.

Words Make a Way Through Fire

Airless. Bare branches
unmoving, small orange wings
flurry the stillness.

    Day break in a new land,
       ageless light breathes home
          everywhere—

Perhaps it is because I have spent years transforming traumatic memory into creative expression that I value a spiritual practice that pays sustained attention to singular, fleeting moments. In order to have a focus for haiku, I must be aware, witness to movements, sounds or visual juxtapositions that might not be obvious at first glance. *Don't forget to be here and now too*, haiku energy seems to say. *Look for beauty no matter the circumstances.*

    Perhaps it is because I respect the consequences of moments that I embrace haiku poems, which gaze deeply if briefly into moments that otherwise might be overlooked. Quiet moments of beauty, moments of wonder, moments of juxtaposition that suggest paradox, nuanced revelation—even these soft moments can be spirals of energy and significance if I pay careful attention. Like a brief plunge into clear spring water from which I emerge full of breath.

    My second week at Istana Cabin brings the gift of a brief rain that sings along the metal roof, slides into the tall cisterns positioned at the cabin corners, and fills them to the brim. I watch water droplets slip from the gutter into the small pool at the mouth of the cisterns, rippling the blue sky now reflected there. I marvel at how much precious water can be collected from a small cabin when a water catchment system is positioned. Later, a male cardinal splashes its red wings in the shallow water glimmering in the pale green cistern.

Haiku Healing

> Rain drop slides into
>   puddled mouth of cistern,
>   ripples blue sky.

>   Cardinal pauses
>   atop the green cistern
>   drinks the sky.

In the midst of solitude, my haiku practice helps me generate courage when I need it. During a powerful storm system that brings lightning strikes close to the cabin, and wind thrumming the metal roof like a flute, I appreciate the companionship of a tiny moth bumping against my lit flashlight. The presence of the moth calms me, and I finally relax into the long blast of storms.

> Little moth flicking my flashlight,
> good to have company
> in this storm.

>   Rain, rain, rain, rain, rain—
>   crescent moon bathes in brimming
>   cistern. Air dries.

Each morning before settling into writing long stretches of prose, I find great pleasure bringing the haiku moment into language. Each morning, my purpose is to honor the vibrancy of the moment resonating from the day before or earlier that morning with as few words as possible. The energy of the moment guides my initial word choices.

    First, I hold the sensory impression of the moment in my mind and body, feeling it as well as seeing it. I hold it like a snapshot-feeling. Then I ask myself: What words do I need to convey this moment to another person? I let those first words come, without concern for syllable count, sketching two or three lines in my journal or on my laptop.

Next, I sit with this sketch, asking: Which words carry the electric bones of the moment? Which words are essential? Which words come closest to recreating the pulse or felt spirit of the passing moment? The playfulness of this creative challenge ripples another wave of wakening.

I discover that articles *the* or *a* often can be dispensed with, as can prepositions and pronouns. Readers can adjust to sentence fragments that coalesce into a vivid whole. Selecting nouns is easy because they name the bird or moth or coyote—the living entity at the heart of the haiku moment. Selecting verbs occupies my longest attention because a well-chosen verb works multidimensionally, conveying movement, texture, sound, as well as the cadence or emotional vibration of an experience. Often I search my thesaurus for verb choices, speaking different ones aloud, feeling how they resonate sonically in my mouth and how they reverberate with nouns already in place. This feels delicious, childlike.

Only after this process of listening and discernment do I pay attention to syllable count. I decide that each haiku should have no more than seventeen syllables overall. The first line, for example, can have six or seven syllables if need be, rather than my insisting the count be five. The syllable count serves the energy of the moment being recreated, line by line. This approach feels truer than strictly assigning five beats to the first line, seven beats to the second, and five beats to the third. If the haiku works with fewer than seventeen syllables, then so be it. If it most truly needs a few more than seventeen, then so be it. Let the haiku spirit decide.

I come to understand how the haiku moment celebrates or emphasizes a relationship between elements, often lifting up a surprising or lovely juxtaposition of elements: the visual delight

Haiku Healing

of a cardinal flashing its bright wings inside a pale green cistern. The song of a coyote as light breaks the dark—how the song awakened the dawn. My senses feel heightened.

> Coyote song strikes
> fire at the edge of night—
> light flares.

Gradually, day by day and haiku by haiku, I feel at home in this region of Texas. Writing haiku daily enhances my awareness of and appreciation for the wildlife living around the cabin. Writing haiku infuses my daily life with a deepened sense of present moment, and a greater alertness, an enlarged capacity for joy. Perhaps there is always a glimmer of beauty, glisten of dew, even amid worry and woe, if I can recognize it. Everything is consequential, even a moth, if I feel its place in the world.

> This land is as flat
> as the desk where I write—same
> fertile ground.

I submerge into this wellspring as prelude to the gravity of prose work to follow. The further I journey into traumatic memory, the more I look forward to beginning each day focused on the beauty of here and now. Writing haiku grounds me. It feels like being returned to the ocean and its beach. The work of shaping this book returns me to key remembered moments, including the moment that Voice spoke both in my mind and in the mirror on February 8, 1974. Now I can feel awe that Voice was aware of me and deeply concerned about my welfare, seeking to help. Now I can feel profound gratitude that it made me a promise: *Cyra, this is going to be very hard! A part of you must hide, a part of you has to deal with what you are about to see. And*

Words Make a Way Through Fire

hear. Smell. I will help you. Remember the dream I sent you a few days ago. Someday, all of you will circle back.

For many years I thought of that presence simply as the voice. It wasn't until recent years that the presence became Voice, with a capital *V*. Who is this Voice? A manifestation of a creative and loving energy in the universe? I believe so. Often, while speaking about the sacred transcendent, I use the words *God* or *Spirit* to name what I mean. But here, in the written context of my fullest life, Voice rings most true.

Voice helped me move through that horrendous evening in real time. Something loving and knowing companioned me. I felt overwhelmed yet not abandoned, aware of transcendence.

A few days earlier, Voice had sought to prepare me by giving me the portentous dream of watching David hurl himself against a moving car. That dream was not of my own making. It flowed from something more knowing than my unconscious mind: a compassionate gift.

Why was I so fortunate to have received such communication, a caution of potential violence soon to come? Words are not sufficient to express my gratitude for this measure of preparation.

I have encountered poems of other poets who seem to know what I am struggling to convey here. Rainer Maria Rilke, an Austrian poet born in Prague in December 1875, would nod knowingly if he could read what I have just written. I believe this when I read this poem from *The Book of Hours*. This is an excerpt of "God speaks to each of us as he makes us" from Rilke's *Book of Hours*:

God speaks to each of us as he makes us,
then walks with us silently out of the night.

These are the words we dimly hear:

Haiku Healing

You, sent out beyond your recall,
go to the limits of your longing.
Embody me.

Flare up like flame,
make big shadows I can move in.

Let everything happen to you: beauty and terror.
Just keep going. No feeling is final.
Don't let yourself lose me.

Nearby is the country they call life.
You will know it by its seriousness.

Give me your hand.

*—Translated from German
by Anita Barrows and Joanna Macy
Book of Hours, I 59*

 The poem's opening image of a Creator not only fashioning our bodies but also breathing sacred perspective into our beings feels like my experience. This Creator makes a promise to walk with us always, acknowledging that our world can be dangerous as well as beautiful. I feel that a specific spiritual purpose or calling can be part of that loving, pre-birth infusion. Guidance from a transcendent presence is alive in me. It has made itself known during moments filled with terror and moments filled with beauty. It has helped me learn how to meet my feelings, move through their shadows and light as I listen inwardly and pay attention outwardly. Voice has even held me in its hand.

 I find myself wondering: When in my life did I first become aware of Voice? How does Voice speak to me or make its presence known? When does Voice make its presence known? Primarily at turning points? Has Voice fulfilled its promise? Have I had a particular part to play in this fulfillment?

During my month at Istana Cabin, these questions pulse like green leaves inside the bark of mesquite trees.

Chapter 12

Voice Speaks Through Dreams and Poems

South Texas Brush Country, March 2020

Dream imagery is a powerful language that Voice uses to speak to me. As I reflect on my life, and the scores of dreams recorded in my journals, three dreams stand out as manifestations of Voice.

I have already shared details of "My Brother David and the Dream," the first dream that felt given by Voice. About twenty years later, while motherhood was still new, I experienced a dream full of spiritual energy. It felt like an intimate encounter with Voice.

Hopefully, the arrangement of words upon the page evokes a sense of movement—being lifted, the parting of clouds, secrets flowing out of me. Short lines allow plenty of white space at the end of lines. This invites taking a pause and taking a breath. In this poem, Voice is imagined as Kind Sight.

Words Make a Way Through Fire

Vision

An unseen hand
  lifts me
    miles into sky
      Clouds part like curtains
        revealing a kind, colossal eye
       Sees into, through me
      with me
       I am filled open wholly to view
      emptied of secrets
     My only desire—stay
    occupied by grace
  Not blink.

I wakened feeling deep peace, feeling that love infuses the universe, and feeling created from and permeated with this love. Transcendent energy had extended itself as a hand to me, and then as a kind eye! I felt absorbed and recognized by this presence while remaining aware of myself as an individual. My flaws, my remorse felt subsumed into loving sight.

While the poem does not indicate it, when the hand of Kind Sight, the hand of Voice, lowered me back to Earth, I was placed in a landscape that resembled northern New Mexico with its white rock formations and glowing red earth. This detail suggests I was returned to this earthly realm with work to do.

One consequence of this dream is that I explore the story of Jesus.

My interaction with the church has been intermittent since childhood. My parents introduced us to Christian thinking and imagery and storytelling cautiously, wary of the prejudice and small-mindedness that can characterize unimaginative congregations. For a few years, my family attended a small, rather progressive Presbyterian-Episcopalian church called Indian

Voice Speaks Through Dreams and Poems

Hill Church located a few miles from our DeMar Road home. My brothers and I sang briefly in the children's choir. I became confirmed as an Episcopalian in eighth grade. A Wednesday morning group for high schoolers centered around conversations started in the church kitchen while we made pancakes. This was where I met Marie, the friend who stayed several nights with me following David's death. David's memorial service took place there, and I was married in its simple, unpretentious sanctuary.

While I liked the social aspect of church membership, I was keenly aware of the absence of the feminine during worship. Referencing God exclusively as Father, as He, distanced me emotionally from scripture and from liturgy. How could a girl relate to the Virgin Mary unless Mary feels intimate and within reach? This doesn't usually happen in a Protestant denomination. Why would a girl want to identify with the other reoccurring Mary, Mary Magdalene, who is usually presented wrongly as a prostitute?

Furthermore, the resurrection of Jesus as a literal event made no sense. Yet, the link between Jesus and love intrigued me, drew me back as an adult to an Episcopalian church in Boerne, Texas. For several years, I served as a lay reader, reading aloud designated prayers, psalms, and passages from scripture during services. I also joined an in-depth and open-minded Bible study course available through this church called Education for the Ministry (EFM).

Through EFM, I discovered a range of images that characterize the mysterious nature of Jesus: Jesus as transparent with God, Jesus as speaker of parables, Jesus as healer, Jesus as transformer of relationships, Jesus as inclusive inviter to the feast, and Jesus as He who sacrifices in order to transcend and reconnect.

I cherished an image of Jesus who is transparent with God, embodying compassionate and healing action in the world. I

Words Make a Way Through Fire

began believing that the point is to embrace the loving, transformative path made clear by the life of Jesus, rather than to worship his memory. I also came to believe that marginalizing people because they do not name their god *Jesus* betrays the transcendent nature of God that is ultimately unsayable.

I discovered Barbara Brown Taylor's book *When God is Silent*, which focuses on the limits of language when we try speaking of God. How do human beings adequately express the infinite mysterious nature of the divine? As Taylor describes it:

> It is precisely our inability to say God that teaches us who God is. When we run out of words, we are very near the God whose name is unsayable. The fact that we cannot say it, however, does not mean we may stop trying.

I appreciate that the sacred is an abundant paradox, represented in the Hebrew Bible as both fire and water. The pillar of smoke by day and pillar of fire by night that leads the Hebrews in Exodus through the desert for forty years toward the Promised Land. When the wandering Hebrews are thirsty, God commands Moses to strike the stone, and hidden clear water pours forth. In Acts of the Apostles, from the New Testament, I love the story about a mighty wind that rushes through a house where the apostles have gathered during Pentecost, soon after the death of Jesus. The wind carries small flames that flicker over the disciples' heads, signifying the presence of the Holy Spirit. Astonished apostles hurry into the streets with a new articulateness, speaking languages that had not flowed before from their tongues.

I tried honoring this fire and water paradox with a poem.

Voice Speaks Through Dreams and Poems

Two Faces, One Name

How is it that You can be
both fire and the wave which extinguishes?

Bright cradle of heat that eats inward from the edges
as well as colorless wave surging ever outward.

Is it all in the momentum, nimbleness:
the way water can flood acres of indigo and rooftops,

the way fire can flare 25 feet up into the cypress—
bursting all boundaries?

The more I contemplated ways of naming God, the more I could pray my own prayers, not only the ones passed along conventionally through liturgy.

I offered my voice as a lay reader for four years; fellow church members repeatedly told me they liked the sound of scripture in my voice. Furthermore, each time I held the chalice of wine during communion as part of my lay reader's role, I felt moved to quiet tears by the beauty of diverse faces pausing to drink.

One Sunday, accompanied by a church member playing a tall drum, I chanted rather than read Psalm 96, "Sing to the Lord a New Song!" Unschooled in chanting, I didn't understand why I felt called to stand before the congregation and trust an unfamiliar way of presenting a psalm. I gave it my all and found that I loved chanting; my whole body resonated deeply with the slow, full vowel tones.

Afterward, I was pleasantly surprised by how many people told me they liked it. Perhaps it triggered an ancient, collective memory of how psalms were originally sung and chanted by the

Words Make a Way Through Fire

Hebrews and later by Christians, their chanting often accompanied by joyful dancing as Spirit poured through their bodies.

Not everyone in the congregation approved of my spiritual independence. My children, of course, were thoroughly mortified as they sat in their choir pews with friends glancing at them askance. My pastor looked red-faced and tight-lipped when I assisted him with communion.

A single word can overthrow, unsettle, and incite great passion. It all depends on the word and the context into which it is released, the readiness of ears.

Several months later, on Easter Sunday, I led the congregation in "Prayers of the People," which was the same script nearly every Sunday, leaving no room for spontaneity or variation. As I stood and began reading the long prayer, the word "Father" seemed decidedly incomplete. I heard myself say aloud what I had long said inwardly: "Father Mother." Repeatedly, each time the text said "Father," I spoke it and added the word "Mother." I did not watch the faces of the congregation; I did not catch the eye of the pastor. I opened my heart to what I heard as a larger linguistic truth.

As we passed the peace a few minutes later, the older woman to my left, also a lay reader, frowned and sizzled with her question, "Father Mother?"

I replied, "Why not?"

When my pastor handed me the communion wafer, he shot me a piercing look. However, compliments expressed by several women afterward gave me heart—none of whom mentioned my use of "Mother."

My family and I enjoyed our Easter brunch, and our week unfolded. Within a few days, a letter arrived from my pastor, one of reprimand. His office had been "inundated" with unsettled calls about my use of "Mother" alongside "Father." His sentences seethed on the page, making clear that I had no right to change the liturgy. My future as lay reader was jeopardized.

Voice Speaks Through Dreams and Poems

I called my pastor to reassure him that I was not launching a campaign; my modification had not been rebelliously calculated to offend nor disrupt. Rather, I had spoken quite spontaneously, in a manner natural to my use of language. The conversation was short; he had little more to say.

I resolved not to read "Prayers of the People" again. While I didn't seek to agitate people with inclusive language, the church didn't have the right to demand that I adhere to their script.

My family and I left this church a few months later, in 2003, when the Episcopal Diocese of West Texas voted at the national convention against installing Gene Robinson, an openly gay and devout man, as bishop for the Episcopal Diocese of New Hampshire. I couldn't condone prejudice against homosexuals by an institution charged with living the message from Jesus to love and accept all persons. I was distressed to learn that when Gene Robinson participated in the formal ceremony consecrating his election as bishop, he had to wear a bulletproof vest beneath his vestments as protection from death threats.

To honor my Easter action of inclusive language, I shaped my feelings of inspiration and indignation into a poem. I slid a copy of the poem under the door of Pastor David's office and walked away from that particular church.

Why My Former Pastor Sent Me a Letter of Reprimand
Because I added "Mother" with "Father" during "Prayers of the People"

One word, the ripple of a single
word spoken during Easter prayer
spoken with tenderness beyond
the bounds of a liturgical script.

How it startles this word,
startles even the one who gave

Words Make a Way Through Fire

it tongue and breath, like running
into the summer ocean for the first time,

embracing the crash of waves
the undercurrent pulling sand
from beneath your feet—
the joy as well as the danger.

You swim into deeper water
ride the waves toward shore
stand again in foaming green
feel something unseen brush

against your legs—shapeless presence
that brushes again and you calculate
how many seconds it would take you
to reach the shore.

But your feet urge peace, do not
be afraid, and you remember
the One, and relax into the mystery
rippling beyond your sight.

In the magnitude of this ocean
there is room. In the vast arc of sky
there is room. In the lift of wooden
arches and the light of altar candles

there is room. No thoughts
are hidden, no desires unknown
to the One and what is spoken
is only the beginning.

Voice Speaks Through Dreams and Poems

～❀～

In addition to giving meaningful dreams, Voice speaks to me through creative process, specifically the writing and shaping of poems. One morning, I woke up with the words "I loved her too much to see her kept in that garden forever. / All that perfection and beauty, after a while it is numbing, / one ripe apple indistinguishable from the next." While I understood this was a poem speaking, I didn't recognize immediately who spoke as *I*. Clearly it wasn't me as Cyra; rather, it was a personality associated with the Judeo-Christian story of Genesis. I realized that it was the serpent speaking. These were opening lines of "Words of the Serpent," the first poem of what evolved gradually into *Listening to Light, Voice Poems*, my second book of poems.

Each poem in *Listening to Light* speaks in first person—uses *I* or *me*—yet, I am not the one who speaks, although I am the writer. Someone other than myself speaks directly as if being channeled through me.

This kind of poem is a monologue or persona poem; I call these collected monologues "voice poems" because they speak a voice that isn't customarily my own. In each one, a character reflects on particular moments or situations. The speaker often explains why he or she or they acted a certain way, what thoughts filled their minds or what feelings unsettled their hearts. These poems, these speakers provide a perspective, an angle of vision on what it means for them to be human (or sentient, in the case of the serpent): their motivations, convictions, feelings, and backstories.

When I write a persona poem, my imagination extends beyond personal life experience. I inhabit the personality imaginatively, and thus emotionally, to create a believable point of view. This creative process allows me a way of seeing how another human feels and responds to challenging circumstances. As I imagine and enter their lives, I identify with an aspect of their being.

Each persona poem allows me to explore some part of my personality, one that relates to the character's life circumstance, even if I haven't lived it directly. Each facilitates a different level of psychological engagement, especially when placing myself inside their skin means confronting emotionally complex events. Each character has a gift to offer me: a realization or unexpected connection. I find this to be a soul-expanding process that increases my capacity for empathy.

After I began *Listening to Light* with "Words of the Serpent," I continued writing poems drawn from Judeo-Christian sacred stories. I was drawn to Old Testament characters such as Eve, Adam, the serpent, Cain, Abel, *and* Cain and Abel's sister. They talked about their relationships with one another and with their creator. One significant revelation for me was the range of names for God that emerged from these characters: Always One, the Name, the Gentle One, the Presence, the Lost One, What Cannot Be Contained, River Unseen.

These poems formed a section of the book called "First Makers." Then I felt moved to write poems that explored Genesis, the New Testament, and the ancient Egyptian story of Isis and Osiris.

Many of the thirty-eight poems that comprise *Listening to Light* allowed me to wrestle with stories from the Judeo-Christian tradition via the lens of my own imagination and life experience. While I regarded the stories as allegories, I often identified with the characters involved. They felt real and instructive. Making these stories my own was important. I would even say that I felt called to do so in large part because of my intimate dream encounter with Kind Sight, which became the poem "Vision."

After writing the points of view of Eve and Adam, especially of Eve, I thought about the brothers, Cain and Abel. I wrote from

Voice Speaks Through Dreams and Poems

Abel's perspective first, intrigued by what the first person to experience death would say about leaving the land of the living alone, entering the afterlife without other human spirits to receive him.

Once Abel had his say, Cain spoke his side of the story. If Abel was the first person to die, then Cain was the first person to commit murder. Not easy to feel sympathetic toward such a person, I thought, as I began filtering his voice through my imagination and experience.

Cain surprised me. He emerged as someone haunted by regret and resentment; but, more so, he emerged as a someone who felt at odds with the world, apart and uneasy, different, cut off from verbal self-expression. As I attuned to his voice, I thought of David's inarticulateness as well as my own isolation when I lack words for emotional experiences. Through the poem, and its need to forge an explanation (if not justification) for why Cain killed his brother, I felt tremendous empathy for all people burdened and alienated by darkness, loneliness, unexpressed anger, brooding, and turbulent silences. I recalled how I once felt strong responsibility for David's death, a sense that has lessened significantly through the years.

Cain Tries to Explain

No easy thing to feel
your brother's warmth drain
away. Your own hands flare
with terrible knowing.
Turn heavy and cold.

I was the first fruit of the other orchard—
the ripe and rotten.
My cry the first to clamor for milk
try our parents.
Winter fevers first to worry.

Words Make a Way Through Fire

Abel came when the earth spilled green.
Something in me gave up
sunlight, went underground.
By the time our sisters were born
moonlight cooled my skin

and roots dusted my hair.
The odd one.
Words for me were
thickness on the tongue.
The worst of it—

watching Mother thin
from the alwaysness of need.
Another woman to help mend
broken bones, savor small joys
would have eased.

Why did I remember that garden—
fields of lilies nodding in blue light,
the glow of stones?
One day I handed Mother
a perfect smooth stone.

She seemed to stop breathing
as she rubbed the stone
against her cheek, her closed eyes.
Then Abel. He darted
into the cave carrying fish to cook.

Startled her awake.
I never planned to kill him.
Later, everything unspoken
shot a burning current up my arms,
grabbled a jagged rock, slammed

Voice Speaks Through Dreams and Poems

his sunburned face—
wanted to stop the moment
I let go.

Not long after I wrote "Cain Tries to Explain," I understood that Cain and Abel have a sister with a story to tell. As this poem flowed through me, I recognized my natural voice and close identification with her emotionally. She, too, is a third child with two older brothers, the eldest of whom had committed a dreadful, fatal act that shocked and disrupted his family. This poem along with the other persona poems written in sequence played a significant part in my healing journey.

Cain and Abel's Sister

I have grown beyond anger,
searching for threads that lead me
past grief and loss to some belonging.

I am nameless, my brothers are famous.
Cain spoke of remembering life in the garden.
It has been for me to remember him and Abel,

the anguish of our parents.
I found Cain beside Abel, holding his cold hand.
Death lingering like a new mist.

When I saw the rock bright with blood
I feared stepping closer.
Cain always spoke loudest with his hands.

Words piled in him like rocks in a river.
Outrage would finally break through.
Regret, its swirling currents, followed later.

Words Make a Way Through Fire

Abel was full of song and laughter.
He loved how summer sank into his skin,
the soft bleating of newborn sheep.

Cain hungered for such easy joy, yet held himself apart,
more comfortable with shadows than light
when we gathered around the fire

to talk, argue, stir the great clay pot.
I would join him sometimes and eat quietly.
He'd smile at me with distant eyes.

I have thought about this as the world has unfolded—
for some of us, life is a broken wheel
and the pieces so scattered

the path can never be made smooth.
Cain and I decided together to bury Abel.
We couldn't let our parents see him,

his face smashed beyond knowing.
We found a place near the best grazing meadows
and fruit trees blooming.

Our hands dug with help of broken rock.
Our digging took us well past sunset.
In the gentle light of moon

we gave Abel to the rich ground
buried him as one might a giant flower bulb,
carefully patting the earth above him.

At dawn we returned to the cave
our hands dark from dirt.
Cain fell to his knees before telling,

Voice Speaks Through Dreams and Poems

led them to the gravesite.
Mother silent until seeing the fruit trees.
Then she began shrieking, hurling fallen apples.

Father finally roused, stilled her arms, gathered
her to him. I did not notice Cain walk away.
He simply vanished into warming air.

He was not there to help me bury our parents.
By then, I was a mother, just beginning
to grasp how grief burrows into bone.

As I mend my children's coverings
I glance into shadows
see again his restless eyes.

Perhaps you do not need to know my name,
you can choose one for me or keep me faceless.
I am everyone who witnesses, remembers,

who loves regardless of the terrible.
I am she whose hands need to carry
a bowl of warm soup into uneasy darkness.

Through the years I have often felt myself standing at Barbara Brown Taylor's "very edge of language" trying to express not only my experience of living with traumatic memory, but also my experience of living in relationship with Voice. Traumatic memory and encounter with Voice are entwined for me. Now I can see that my encounters with Voice allow me to grow creatively into and beyond traumatic memory, largely through writing poetry. Through my poems, I enter traumatic memory safely, absorb and release much of its frightful energy, restore my fractured and destabilized center. Through my poems, I integrate fractures into a powerful wholeness, feel infusions of courage, and receive images, metaphors, and words that help me speak my most layered and complete truth. During the process of making poems, I feel held by Voice.

Poetry allows me to speak multidimensionally, weaving feeling, bodily sensations, and thoughts into language as well as spiritual energy. My understanding, what I think of as my inner and layered sight, is best conveyed through poems, formed primarily from imagery and feeling, from the rhythms and resonances of words as well as from the pauses around the words.

I love shaping poetic lines along with shaping sentences. By taking a sentence and allowing it to form a series of vertical lines for a poem, I pay more attention to each individual word of the sentence. I slow down and experience each word. I hear them speak more fully. As I pay them more attention, they become more real.

My eyes have always been very weak. Both David and I inherited our mother's myopic eyes. I once overheard Mother say to a friend, "In the years before glasses, I would have been the village idiot, or else fallen down a well." I resolved that I would listen well to compensate for my limited vision.

When I entered first grade, I sat near the back of the classroom where I had no trouble copying words and simple arithmetic problems from the blackboard. But the distinctions between "3" and "8" and "e" and "c" grew blurred as the school year progressed. Sometimes the blackboard appeared to be underwater, the words swimming in place. The grown-ups talked about my increasing number of mistakes; even then, I liked thinking of myself as a good student, one who got the answers right most of the time. My teacher moved me forward a few rows, which helped for a while. Then the words rippled again. I ended up in the front row and still felt as if I were

Voice Speaks Through Dreams and Poems

fishing, until I wore my first pair of eyeglasses—pale blue with navy rhinestones in the square corners.

The simple act of removing my glasses effaced the material world. Without glasses, my own hand dissolved two feet from my face. The world was a tricky place that had to be taken largely on faith. Anything halfway across the room might as well have been a continent away; it didn't exist unless I bumped into it.

Curiously, it was during first grade that I wrote my first poem about a bluebird singing in my mind. As I lost acuity of physical sight, I simultaneously felt myself named as a writer, someone who transforms inner sight into "plain sight" through words.

Although I didn't fully comprehend it at the time, I grew up aware that inner sight, both arising from imagination and from intuition, was real and powerful and impossible to predict. I remember being ten and visiting a family whose daughter went to school with David and me. A gymnast, Christa could do backbends and roundoffs as easily as if she were walking down a sidewalk, her long dark ponytail cascading behind her like a waterfall. At one point, I went to the bathroom. As I closed the door, I had an odd vision, a premonition: Christa's little brother bolting into the bathroom, looking at me and laughing, then dashing out. I decided to test the vision without risk of embarrassment, so I stood fingering the soap and waited. About ten seconds passed, then Kevin burst through the door. He looked at me, glanced at the toilet, turned and ran giggling out to the hallway. I closed the door again, locked it and finished my business, thinking how strange this sequence of events had been.

When I was thirteen and a freshman in high school, I dated a red-haired junior my parents didn't like. I didn't much like Ted either, but I was very insecure with thick glasses, stringy brown hair, and newly freed of braces. Having the eye of an older boy made me feel that I had some sex appeal, some power in being female.

Words Make a Way Through Fire

One Sunday, David drove some friends and me to Ted's house to see his newborn German shepherd puppies. It was a muddy day and Ted's mother didn't want a bunch of teenagers tramping through her house. In order to access the garage from outside, Ted had to back his red Impala away from the door. In high spirits, I jumped on the front hood of the car, leaned against the windshield, resting my feet on a metallic hood ornament with a long-spiked shape. As Ted slowly drove backward, I saw myself sliding forward and into the prong. It was like watching a brief video. A few seconds later, Ted accelerated suddenly and I slid into the spike, which plunged through my jeans and pierced my thigh. David had to drive me home immediately so our parents could get me to the emergency room. I spent the afternoon at Mercy Hospital waiting to be stitched up by a physician whose hands shook as he stitched, leaving me with a clumsy scar.

I have lived long enough to undergo wondrous eye surgery and am liberated now from thick lenses that were once an extension of David and me. I have learned how to reckon with the physical world in a more direct way. I learned to deal with the yellow snake with brown markings down its spine coiled in my living room that I mistook briefly for a jump rope.

One great joy of having far-reaching, outward sight as well as intuitive, inner sight is being able to relax fully while swimming. Over the years, my swimming life settled into a year-round practice; I need to swim at least a mile, three or four times a week to feel emotionally balanced. My body and spirit crave swimming. The solid world slides away as I enter the world of rhythm and flow where sounds are muffled, and I feel beyond gravity. I get contemplative, allowing the seamless rhythm of arms, legs, and breath working together to lead me, letting my intuitive mind glide forward. As I swim, solutions arise for problems with poems I am writing or questions relevant to my teaching.

Voice Speaks Through Dreams and Poems

A few years following my poem "Vision," and following my first round of eye surgery that allowed me to see clearly beyond a few inches, I experienced perfect swimming. While staying at Laity Lodge, a retreat center owned by the H. E. Butt Foundation and located on a two-thousand-acre Hill Country property, I swam a private fork of the Frio River. Water that flowed freshly from nearby springs had a lovely silken feel. I spent hours immersed, often closing my eyes and swimming blind, feeling the water flow through me as I flowed through the water.

Swimming the Frio Near the Headwaters

Dive into jade
    wave upon pure wave
        churning up from below
            a quiet you can trust

long as you understand
    that the darkness means depth
        means rowing your body
        toward shore

Let eyes close
    see with your body
        even while turning for air
            Feel the river swim you

release the deep gentle
    be within
        perfect silken silence
            blessed rhythm of limbs

    lasting oneness with green.

Words Make a Way Through Fire

❧

Impressed by this spiritual experience of water, I arranged to stay for five days in a stone cottage called the Quiet House on a remote hilltop in the Frio Canyon. Dan took several days off from work to care for the children who were ages seven and five years old. It is here that I wrote much of the earliest version of this story called "Brother/Sister." It was late November. A warm Texas winter so far. A few wooded miles from the Quiet House is the Frio River. As preparation for swimming during a chilly season, I purchased a special "skin," a thin wet suit: black with a silver *S* on the front that includes a detached hood, boots, and gloves.

I was eager to swim Blue Hole again, an especially beautiful part of the Frio River that wasn't blue at all. It was liquid jade, except in the shade, and then it looked so green as to appear nearly black. The river was narrow but very deep, thirty to forty feet deep. From hundreds of feet above Blue Hole, from the rim of the Frio Canyon looking down, I easily imagined that—once upon a time—limestone layers on either side of the river were connected; then came a great wrenching, a divide in the stone. Water gushed upward from below and filled in the deep, narrow crack.

Although apprehensive, I enacted my plan of winter swimming on a sunny afternoon. I carried my gear several miles down the side of the canyon, across the dam, and along a gravel road. Late afternoon shadows darkened a large portion of Blue Hole.

As I stepped into my taut, black skin, a red-tailed hawk glided low overhead, giving me encouragement. Not sure what to do with the long black cord that allowed me to zip up the back zipper unassisted, I left it to dangle outside of the skin as I put on my hood, boots, and gloves. Encased in black, I entered the dark water.

Voice Speaks Through Dreams and Poems

It was decidedly chilly. My feet felt heavy even in lightweight boots. I missed the ease of bare feet. I missed the sensuality of my skin directly against the water. Yet, I was glad to swim—a slice of night gliding through green.

I thought about Jacob wrestling all night with a stranger whom he understands as a representative of God, an angel perhaps. Although something of a scoundrel, Jacob receives first a blessing, and then pays a price for his sacred thrashing—a wound in his thigh that causes him to limp the rest of his life. I thought about the scar on my thigh, how it ached sometimes when I recalled high school years. I swam with my head held up, observing the limestone cliffs and vast sky, awestruck by the dark water.

Abruptly, *something*—probably a giant catfish—tugged at the long black cord dangling beneath me. Pulled me under the river's surface. Held me there. When I looked below, only a vague shape was visible. As I grew fearful, it released me. I came up for air, pulled up the cord, and tucked it into the front of my suit. I felt vulnerable yet protected as I continued swimming.

I swam until my bones noticed the chill, then I glided to the ladder and climbed out. Shivering as I unpeeled my synthetic skin, I stood awhile in a small patch of sunlight. The long walk back to the Quiet House continued warming my bones.

The next morning, I discovered a book on the shelf of the Quiet House called *The Kingdom Within* written by Jungian analyst and Episcopal priest John A. Sanford. This passage stood out to me:

> God is as personal to us as our own inner creative process. Creativity comes when we make contact with the living contents of the inner world—the inner fish—and bringing them to the surface, give them expression . . . in the creatively led life, we act in the image of God.

Words Make a Way Through Fire

Sanford's language, his use of "inner fish," in light of yesterday's experience with presumably an unseen fish, resonated powerfully. My life continues feeling like a manifestation of what Sanford articulates. It is through my creative expression, my poem-making, that I feel most consistently connected to Voice. Voice knows me and has implanted a guiding purpose within my soul. There is specific work for me to do. The work is not always easy. It has included bearing fiery witness as well as trusting deep waters—all of which emerges as poems, the living contents of my inward world: my "inner fish." The more I listen, the more clearly I see.

Winter Swimming

"So now, not only in my presence but much more now in my absence, work out your own salvation with fear and trembling..."

—Philippians 2:12

Alone at the river in winter, I step into synthetic skin,
tug it over my ankles, up the right leg then the left.
Snug at my wrists, the blackness eases

toward my shoulders. Up with the zipper
that begins below my waist in the back,
metal teeth clacking as I pull the long line,

feel tightness swaddle ribs, throat.
Slip on lightweight boots, gloves, black hood.
I shiver, taking on a disguise I don't recognize,

don't know the limits of its warmth
as I turn toward this curve of river
where the deep falls so dark I can't see

Voice Speaks Through Dreams and Poems

through it and am pulled beyond reason
to trust. Why must I swim this frigid water?
Suppose God is a great fish waiting

along the lowest shelf of limestone?
Something is always given, something always asked.
My hands long to peel off the gloves, scoop the cold,

make it feel warm as summer.
How must I look from the cliffs above,
a sliver of night knifing through jade?

How must I look from below, zipper line
trailing like an afterthought?
Fire fades inside my bones

but this skin keeps swimming me
farther from shore, toward where the Frio widens.
As I turn on my back, glide, something seizes the line,

pulls me under, holds me halfway
between sinking and rising.
Too deep to see underneath except

a gigantic flare of something not quite fin.
I hear silence: *All is well.*
Look up. Notice the waves.

The line stays taut.
I look, see how light stirs
the surface into small waves.

Stillness fills,
sends peace pushing
outward like cells of new skin.

Words Make a Way Through Fire

Will the miracle be amphibious:
gift of gills as well as lungs?
To live fearless in water and on land?

I hardly feel the ascent
until my own breath breaks the waves,
steers me toward shore.

Slow fingers remove hood, gloves, boots,
unpeel the rubber suit which flops inside out.
Touch my own warmth emptied there,

a kind of lining, momentary press of self,
skin beneath the skin beneath
a bareness I can't live without—

During my stay at the Quiet House, I took a break from my reading and writing to walk the small labyrinth adjacent to the cabin and made by hand with stones found on the property. As I walked its curves and turned its small bends, ending up in the center, I meditated on the words of a psalm that I had just read.

The urge to sing several lines of the psalm welled up within me. At first I sang tentatively, more from my mouth and throat than with my core. The urge to sing loudly, to give all of myself to saying and chanting the words was undeniable. As I did so, my body and soul vibrated, resonated. Some final deep scream, perhaps the one I swallowed the moment I first saw David aflame, finally found a safe, beautiful way to emerge.

Voice Speaks Through Dreams and Poems

Quiet House Epiphany

Something deep within
has been all too quiet.
It must break loose,
breathe this sky,
this clearing now—
let it loose

Bless my soul, oh my lord
and all that is within me,
bless your holy name—

the leaves of the live oak
trees flutter, lean in
closer as I chant

Bless my soul, oh my lord
and all that is within me,
bless your holy name—

allow my voice to be LOUD
sound, sound, sound
allow such sound

OH, OH
soul,
holy soul

vowel sounds hold the agony,
hold the howl I could not sound
years ago—no time
cries of pain
yours,
nothing I can do to save you,

Words Make a Way Through Fire

*Bless my soul, oh my lord
and all that is within me,
bless your holy name—*

I will not restrain—
bless me, bless this pain
his and mine,

become echo
released
reverberate these canyon walls,

free.

Chapter 13

Becoming Owl-Woman

While staying at the Quiet House years ago and then years later at Istana Cabin, I experienced owls as important presences. I was meditating on a hammock in the yard of the Quiet House just before dusk. The air stirred slightly. I opened my eyes as a great horned owl glided right past me, landing long enough to clutch a sparrow and fly off with it. While I felt pity for the sparrow who uttered a single cry, I also felt granted a remarkable sight. The chance to notice the gliding, silent owl had been a fleeting moment; I could have kept my eyes closed and missed it.

While staying at Istana, a great horned owl became a recurring presence. I heard it calling nearby for several evenings before sighting the owl. It was a transitional time, day turning into night. I sat on the bench swing of the west porch appreciating the bright sunset colors. The air flickered behind me, as if wings had just folded into a feathered body. I turned and spotted the silhouette of the owl perched on a metal beam of the hay barn.

This owl became a focal point for several haiku. Here is one:

Owl calls from edge
of my hearing—distant
word I need just now?

Words Make a Way Through Fire

I thought about an unfinished poem involving owls that described a recent dream:

I am summoned to a distant cabin to heal someone gravely ill. To cover the distance quickly, I must fly—become an Owl-Woman. To prepare for the flight, I summon fellow healers to accompany me on my inaugural flight as healer. We perform a ritual, affirm that our intentions are pure, then leap into the air, not knowing how else to become owls. Our wings and talons spontaneously emerge, and we fly across mountains to a lone cabin where we land, returning to our human shape before we enter the cabin. Curiously, as I enter the room to meet the person who has summoned me as a healer, I wake up. I don't see my "patient."

Transforming from human to owl form, experiencing flight, and vividly witnessing the mountainous landscape felt like an initiation into my practice of poetic medicine. The dream felt like a magical gift from Voice, a gift that was mysterious and unfinished because the ending was unclear.

Soon after dreaming, I drafted a poem to embody the dream narrative. I wanted to preserve the sensation of flying as much as possible, along with the feeling of ritual that served as prelude to flying.

I didn't know how to end the poem. At first, I thought that the person gravely ill who had summoned me might be David. Finally, we were having our reunion. When I shaped that ending into words, it felt flat and contrived. Something deeper wanted to surface, but I couldn't yet sense it. I deleted the reference to David and set the poem aside, letting it breathe.

It took the presence of an owl at Istana Cabin, and accepting myself as a healing influence, to see how the narrative truly ends. The person who had summoned me and waited for my healing touch was my sixteen-year-old self. She was ready to be formally retrieved and welcomed. She was ready to fly home with me and take her place within the larger circle of healing poetry practitioners. Allowing this ending to flow through felt deeply satisfying, as if the "circling back" image given to my sixteen-year-old self by Voice had been completed, fulfilled. Each time I read this poem, I feel a surge of joy.

Owl-Woman Dream

One morning you receive a message:
across the mountains another woman
is gravely ill. Will you journey
to the bedside of an ailing stranger?

You do not advertise your healing services
so this summons surprises. *Of course I will come,*
you reply by rubbing together two stones.
Their spark of light signals two friends

who immediately appear. "Let us hasten,"
you say. "We must travel a great distance,
so we will become owls." The three of you
stand in a circle around a blue basin of water,

and declare that your intent is pure as water
fresh from hidden springs. Then you leap into
the bright air, not knowing how else to become owls.
Wings unfold from shoulders and backs,

your bodies layer with golden feathers, and
your talons still bear turquoise rings.

Words Make a Way Through Fire

You ascend, lifted by a spiraling updraft
which sends you flying southeast, high over

green mountains and rain-fast rivers.
The sensation of flying feels natural, effortless.
Rabbits bound across a grassy field,
surprised to see owl-women flying.

Mountain ranges fold swiftly into one another
as you gain speed and height. A valley
emerges, and you spiral down
toward a small stone house. You land

upon the front porch, taking your first step
as woman again. You enter the house, and follow
the scent of sage down a long hallway,
floorboards creaking.

As you step into her room, the ailing woman
gazes at you with your sixteen-year-old face.
"You have come at last," she says.
"The voice in the mirror promised

that you would circle back for me someday."
Speechless, you nod and step towards her;
she rises. As you take her hand,
everything is remembered and forgiven.

Already, she knows how to fly.
Already, she knows the way home;
side by side you fly back over the mountains
in a whirlwind of feathers.

Becoming Owl-Woman

My recovery from David's suicide has been a lifelong journey, a journey that continues as my understanding of how my healing can serve other people expands. Crucial to my inner transformation has been the creative process of poem-making.

Poem-making has enabled me to shift gradually from feeling fractured and anxiously preoccupied by traumatic memory to feeling whole, revitalized, and purposeful. Poem by poem, I have learned to hear and trust what the poet William Butler Yeats referred to as the "deep heart's core"—that part of us that is inherently whole and creative by nature. This inner "place" is where Voice breathes and offers images that emerge sometimes during dreams, other times while making poems, and when I seek prayerful guidance.

I believe that Voice implanted within me a deep love for and relationship with poetry that was activated when I was very young: activated by my mother's voice reading aloud stories and poems, activated by my father's voice telling stories around a campfire, and activated by my sensory experience of the ocean during childhood. Voice seems to have known all along that I had the capacity to transform my traumatic witness into a creative journey. Voice has guided me toward poetry as an essential means of liberation from psychic devastation.

"Poetry is the voice of the soul, whispering, celebrating, singing even," said poet Carolyn Forché. As the voice of the soul, poetry connects holistically to human beings—body, bone, blood, emotion, dream, thought, memory, spirit. One of the ancient arts, poetry is the most articulate and layered form of verbal self-expression, enabling us to express feelings, thoughts, physical sensations, and memories simultaneously.

Words Make a Way Through Fire

"Poetry is a kind of multidimensional language," writes Laurence Perrine in *Sound and Sense*. He goes on to say that poetry has at least four dimensions. He continues:

> If it is to communicate experience, poetry must be directed at the whole person, not just their understanding. It must involve not only their intelligence but also their senses, emotions, and imagination. Poetry, to the intellectual dimension, adds a sensuous dimension, an emotional dimension, and an imaginative dimension.

Poetry is a form of music, a kind of singing as Forché observes, where cadence and voice, sonorousness and silence are woven into the word-flow. When a poem is shaped with attention to how words are placed on the page (line breaks and stanza breaks—pauses where breath is invited, where mental reflection is invited), poetry is also a form of visual art. When spoken aloud with a mindful voice or performed with an attuned body, poetry is an embodied art.

For all these reasons, lyric poetry has natural healing properties not always found in other kinds of writing: clear and strong images that readers can inhabit, words whose sounds and rhythms sing to one another like music, contemplative pauses that summon reflection and new insights, fresh mental sight that unfolds as an extended metaphor is explored. Poetry brings a comforting orderliness to the process of wrestling with traumatic experiences. The poem on the page creates a safe holding space for facing painful as well as portraying beautiful experiences. When poem-making becomes a sustained practice, the once traumatized poet can build an inner strength, strength necessary to meet life challenges and opportunities with resilience and hopefulness, with perspective and empathy.

Becoming Owl-Woman

I understood much of this when I began teaching composition and then poetry writing at St. Mary's University in August 2000. After completing my master's degree in English, I was drawn to teach poetry writing and composition at the college level. My first thought was to apply at the University of Texas at San Antonio's main campus located just a few miles from my home, where I had received my graduate degree. Then I was invited to talk about *What the Body Knows*, my first book of poems, at St. Mary's University where my editor at that time, Karen Narvarte, served as faculty.

I thoroughly enjoyed my conversation with Karen's students. They were inquisitive, respectful, and appreciative. After class, Karen and I were talking outside of Garni Science Building when Voice said, *Cyra, I need you here.* As it had been a while since Voice had spoken audibly to me, I looked behind me half expecting to see Voice standing nearby.

I took a slow breath to quiet my surprise and asked Karen whether or not the English Department needed adjunct faculty. "Yes," she answered and told me whom to contact. Within two months, I met with the chairwoman of the department and was hired to teach two composition courses for the Fall 2000 semester.

Although I had a tremendous amount to learn about teaching, and often felt overwhelmed by what I didn't know, I loved interacting with students as they developed a more coherent and articulated writing voice, one that they valued. Creating a supportive environment within which people discovered their voices as writers through writing and revision brought me deep satisfaction. Seeing students turn struggles to express their thoughts into meaningful essays and poems, while gaining confidence and gratification, gave me joy.

Working closely with students as they shaped and revised multiple drafts of essays, narratives, or poems, I came to know my students pretty well. Every semester, I conducted individualized conferences, during which students often confided their struggles with life as well as with their writing. Personal stories emerged that related to their struggle to write, especially details about how life challenges impacted their academic work.

Following several years of teaching, I understood that during any given semester, some students were being diagnosed with depression, while others were adjusting to medication changes and dealing with bouts of insomnia. Their mental concentration could become impaired as latent depression or anxiety emerged. Energy for studies and taking major tests or writing lengthy research essays could become compromised. They might start missing classes or deadlines for turning in assignments, not due to laziness, rather because they were overwhelmed. These behaviors, these responses to chronic and situational depression, impeded their academic engagement and performance. This, along with fear of stigma when asking for help, could derail not only a student's semester, but also an entire academic career.

Experience quickly taught me that approximately 25 percent of students in any given course that I taught were coping with depression, either situational or chronic. While I arrived at this estimate of 25 percent by 2005, a few years into teaching, a study released during the summer of 2015 by the *Chronicle of Higher Education* affirmed my observation.

I was driving home from St. Mary's on a September day in 2015, listening to National Public Radio, when I heard Robin Wilson, an investigative reporter for the *Chronicle of Higher Education*, being interviewed for a program called "On Point." During this interview, Wilson said that 58 percent of college counseling centers in the United States had reported a significant increase in clinical depression among their students over the past decade. She reported that 25 percent of students who made use of college counseling centers were already taking psychiatric medication. College counseling centers were struggling to meet the increased demand for counseling services for depression and for anxiety.

It became increasingly clear to me that poetic medicine could help some students struggling with depression find relief from symptoms such as self-isolation and self-alienation. I believed that poems which give voice to a student's daily struggle with chronic depression could both lighten their hearts and provide a tool for communicating their inner experience with depression to family members, friends, coworkers, and professors—people who mean well but often don't understand how to effectively support a persistently depressed person. As I discovered as David's sister, and then again as a college instructor, depressed students need help finding a language that conveys their inner landscape in such a way that the people who regularly interact with them can appreciate. They need an effective way to share their emotional experience and psychological reality.

By August 2015, I had been teaching at St. Mary's University for about fourteen years, primarily composition courses and poetry writing courses, with some literature courses as well. My evolution as a university instructor had evolved to the point where I then required students to keep personal journals. Each week, they wrote in their journals for at least an hour as a way of making contact with their emotional and imaginative selves, using informal writing as self-discovery, catharsis, slowing down long enough to focus their thoughts, and recording simple moments of beauty. I never read their journals; instead they gave me weekly personal journal logs. At the end of the semester, students wrote an argument for or against the requirement of keeping the personal journal. The vast majority of students wrote eloquently about the specific benefits of the requirement, linking their argument to how the practice of journaling supported their mental or emotional health.

My accumulation of student testimonials that affirmed how a writing practice as simple as personal journaling improved their mental health felt significant. Simultaneously, I observed how helpful it was to students psychologically and academically when their relationship to their writing voice was strengthened, either through a highly individualized composition course or a poetry writing course. I was convinced that writing as a self-care, stress-reducing, and wellness tool helped many students become more successful and better able to comprehend and communicate their inner lives.

My belief in the value of writing for therapeutic purposes led me in 2015 to complete an intensive certification program as a practitioner of poetic medicine through The Institute for Poetic Medicine, founded by John Fox, a highly regarded practitioner of poetic medicine. I felt called to learn even more than my personal experience had taught me about creating spaces where individuals can experience poetry as healer and journaling as wellness.

I was drawn to this multiphased certification program because I wanted to be of greater service to my students. I wanted further insight into how I might structure writing practices as transformative experiences for students both inside and outside of the classroom. And I was drawn to this certification program because, once again, Voice nudged me to apply.

During the first, most introspective phase of the training program, I wrote the following poem, pausing at one point in the writing process to study a diagram of the inner ear, and learn names of the tiny bones.

Becoming Owl-Woman

Scientist of Silences
for my brother David

Only God and the pine trees
saw what I saw: you burning
out there in the open.

Everything happened so fast,
and then: the lasting silence,
the accusatory silence,

silence of what I had not said
in the kitchen, before I turned away,
left you alone with that voice.

What life form might you be now:
dust inside the belly of a sea turtle,
a boy dodging bicycles in Pakistan?

For years, I dissected the body of silence:
unraveled vessels of the circulatory system,
journeyed the auditory nerve from memory to the ear,

named the tiny bones nestled near the eardrum:
malleus, incus, and stapes, traced the deep spiral
of cochlea with my finger.

Now, when young men and women walk the long,
university hallway on the fourth floor of Chaminade,
stop at my door—eyes burning with questions,

I bid them enter.
As they word their way from silence,
give form and edge to the dreadful unsaid,

light dusts the leaves of pecan trees,
paper butterflies turn slowly above my desk,
their invisible breeze soft as breath upon my neck.

Words Make a Way Through Fire

❧

When I entered the final phase of completing my certification as a practitioner of poetic medicine in 2015, I had been offering weekly, therapeutic poetry writing circles at the university for about two years. I also had facilitated circles for hospice volunteers and staff. While I had gained confidence as a facilitator for small groups, I did not yet think of myself as a healing presence. I understood that by listening carefully to students or to anyone expressing their inner life, my empathic presence and response could help people feel visible and valued.

When I considered the word "practitioner" in relationship to "poetic medicine," I understood how my practice of poem-making had generated healing through the decades. I knew how to engage with writing as a generative means that breaks my silence and isolation even as a redbud blossom breaks through bark in the spring. In this sense, I saw myself as a tree blossom. I did not yet see myself also as the stem that connects the blossom-turned-leaf to the tree. I hadn't shown myself that I can hold sustained, therapeutic space for another person breaking through their layers of isolation, their bark.

Before I could embody the practice of "holding space" for someone beyond an individual student conference, I needed to imagine it. I needed to live and feel it as well as think through the concept. I needed the "right" metaphor, one that was relevant, applicable, and spiritually meaningful to me. I asked myself: What might it feel like to be the person holding safe space for someone else as they confront something powerful and troubling within themselves, gain a new understanding of it, and by so doing, rebirth their relationship to that memory or those feelings? By rebirthing their relationship to this troubling thing, they also rebirth their sense of self; my own experience had taught me this. This process of encounter was a kind of season, a season of rebirthing their identity, a season that takes weeks and months.

I read about bark, what it is formed from and how it is possible for a blossom or a leaf to push through the plant cellulose into open air. My imagination was seeded; the following poem emerged slowly, gradually, feeling its way.

Stem

1
Do you know dormancy, stricture
of living tightly: tiny bud wedged

within winter branch, not yet summoned?
Such restriction has its beauty, long as

it is brief, seasonal. Such innerness offers
a dark cocoon, haven for clarifying hunger.

Snug as it is, it isn't airless.
Be alert for scent of fruit,

signal that the calling time is near.
You will feel yourself loosening,

pulling away from vagueness, gaining edge.
Your strength guides as you arise

through layers of bark,
open fully into air.

You will see your own flesh,
green and delicately robust,

feel deep hunger turn into light.

2
You think you have finished your work

until you feel again the churning, again the emergence—
you extend, unfold a leaf, which also leans into light.

You are stem. Place of connection
between spring leaf and branch:

the inward turned outward, offering holding
space for others to seek fruition.

As I shaped and revised the poem, I recognized that the first section of "Stem" expressed my personal practice of poem-making as medicine: my inner life as refuge where I find the quiet and resolve needed to push through resistance and self-silencing into light, air, poetry. This outgrowth is enough for a while. Then, I recognized that the second section portrayed my calling to grow another segment of my being, to hold creative space for other "leaves" who want to move from winter into spring.

The metaphor of stem was a landscape around which the poem revealed its insight. It showed me that being the person who holds trustworthy, creative space for others has a sacred responsibility toward that other person. This is not to be done lightly. It takes an inward calm and yet an alert energy, honorable intent, and feeling grounded within myself. Writing this poem made me aware that my practice of offering poetic medicine for other people was built on my practice of poetic medicine for myself. In order to sustain a practice intended to serve others, I would need to continue my lifelong practice of churning, discerning, and emergence through phases of writing.

The spring semester of 2016 was an especially powerful season of spiritual growth. During a series of January days, I

Becoming Owl-Woman

experienced what I came to understand as psychological labor pains. An unknown, primal energy broke through my core and enlarged my awareness. It was an intensely physical experience. Imagine having a spiral that moves upward and downward at different times suddenly take root inside you.

This spiral carved a deeper channel for healing energy to move through me when called on for the purpose of healing. But I didn't understand this at first. My initial sensation was feeling incredibly disoriented as I felt myself inhabiting an ancient time and space, as well as my current life.

I entered a spiraling energy unbound by human time that was intense and visionary. Actually, it entered me without notice in the midst of teaching, in the midst of transactions at the bank, in the midst of working at my desk. It first happened during my night class when I was elaborating why I required keeping a personal journal as part of the course. Suddenly I saw, beyond the walls and the students seated at long tables before me, a cave lit by campfire. I sensed the spirits of other people whose faces I couldn't distinguish in the subdued firelight. I was both here and now *and* there and then.

Such sensory disorientation took place multiple times in various places over the course of about a week, causing me to describe my inner experiences to my husband. It felt creative and soulful, though emotionally overwhelming. Given the specter of mental illness in my family, I wanted Dan to keep an eye on me in case I crossed some unseen line into sustained confusion.

While I was aware that my consciousness was experiencing upheaval, I also felt Voice steadfastly with me, reassuring me when I needed it most. As I look back on this now, I see that I was becoming Owl-Woman then, midwifing Cyra who offers writing as healing for other people, in deeper, more intentional, and diverse ways.

Words Make a Way Through Fire

As I write this, I see that if there was ever a particular season when Voice manifested in a palpable manner the promise made to me in the mirror, it was this time. I realigned inwardly, gained access to a new vibration of spiritual energy that flowed through me from a Larger Source beyond me. This attunement impacted me physically, mentally, as well as spiritually. I think it would have overwhelmed me had I not continued swimming and poem-making, practices that helped me to maintain center within the whirling of unfamiliar intensity.

Profound and beautiful transformations took place for various students taking classes with me during these two semesters as well, transformations that amazed them as well as me. The following journal entries describe the mysterious and marvelous unsettling that I lived and observed over a series of months.

January 9, 2016

Where Does the Circle Begin?

This circle begins
as a thread from my heart,
and the desire that love
for others will open me,
extend
through my arms, my words
into this air—

where breath & images & memories
of all who gather
form

an intricate crossroads,
an intricate weave of unfolding spirals:
palpable yet invisible.

Becoming Owl-Woman

January 10, 2016

In my dream I am staying in my old bedroom at DeMar, a bedroom that now belongs to Dad and Janet. I find it strange that I have displaced Dad and Janet from their room which was once my room. I step into the small bathroom which was once my bathroom. As I step into the bathroom of memory, I catch the scent of David's smoky, burnt-flesh presence. He is not there, just the powerful scent of an old resonant moment. I wash hands at the sink that was once my sink, and water spills onto the floor.

January 14, 2016

I want to be fluid the way light
is fluid when it rides the back
of a river, the way an orange
is fluid as it rolls across
a marble floor to the heart of
a church sanctuary, like a tiny comet
blazing a momentary path &
beheld as unforgettable.
I want to be fluid the way time
is fluid when it melts in fire, hearth
of your body—chakra of the heart,
core of your energy,

intricate threads of body's web
when time melts and you feel
yourself to be in five maybe six places
at once—part memory, part now, part future—
the only ground beneath you is wonder,
question, astonishment.
You kneel to feel anything solid—carpet

Words Make a Way Through Fire

or marble or pine needles—
while the sound that pours
like vibrating water
from your throat, chest, pelvis
keeps you from levitating—

January 15, 2016

These Spirals that Surge

The classroom window is closed
yet the brilliant wind enters, silent
and all-seeing,
        pours through my forehead
        flares light through my spine,
        my body now a radiant flute

              what instrument
              have I become?

        where is this space
        where am I being
        played, memory replayed
        from a former life?

              Whose presence
              seeks to break through?

Coming up for air—
Where? Who is there
gathered around the flames,
who is there, who calls
Am I being summoned forward
or back to something

Becoming Owl-Woman

    I have already seen,
      yet have no name for?

I fall through a portal, throb
in my forehead, expanding space
between my eyes—fall

am caught by a window of sight—
familiar way of seeing
dissolving, unraveling

vibration uncoiled,
holding me in its throb
sounding, sounding
releasing golden coils of sound

        I no longer hold the circle
          the circle holds me
            I live its vibrations
am I releasing
      am I receiving

Why do I sense / see / feel myself
to be in a cave,
healing ceremony—
deep spiritual energy
souls of young women glowing?

So ancient & familiar
my body a channel of reverence
remembering
realigning with a deeper root.

Words Make a Way Through Fire

January 16, 2016

My mind feels mentored by the sky—
spaciousness, expanse
invitation by its constant presence
to persist through
the cracks,
hold many glazes of light
as well as turning pools of shadow

my heart feels called to summer wings,
become the falcon,
traveler of spirals. Open
wings to trust
embrace the unwinding.

January 17, 2016

It is difficult to explain more directly what has been happening to me this past week. I will try speaking it as more of a story now that I have written about its sensations, its images, and energy, needing the spacing and pauses and breaths of poetic lines to try, try to convey this mystery in whose grip I have been and perhaps will always be living.

Tuesday evening during the first gathering of my weekly night class at St. Mary's, standing before a mix of graduate and undergraduate students, and bringing closure to our first class together, I felt seized by a huge wave. I felt an internal infusion of energy pouring from my forehead, down my spine, along the back of my legs. The walls around the room dissolved, and I thought we were all inside a cave. Students and friends from various times in my life felt vaguely present, even as I maintained touch with the students before me now.

Becoming Owl-Woman

I held onto my words although I sat down, verging on dizziness. It wasn't so much dizziness as it was riding huge ripples of energy. The students didn't seem alarmed, so I assumed that only I was experiencing this strange reality.

When class ended, Gina was the last student to leave the room. She had been seated on my right at the end of the table and had barely spoken. Now, she slowly gathered her things as if lost in deep thought. Her blonde hair fell loosely around her expressionless face. I stood up, holding onto the back of my chair, and said good night to her. She said good night to me with a masklike face and eyes filled with sorrow.

I moved slowly, gathering my books and papers, tucking them into my backpack, taking stock of my physical and mental balance. Was I still pulsating? Yes, but softly now. Did I think I could manage the twenty-five-minute drive home through the winter darkness? I thought so.

Was there a student at the table with powerful, spiritual energy? Was there a student in this class with whom I am meant to deeply connect, support, learn from, be amazed by? Could it be the young woman with grieving eyes and frozen face? I realized I needed to keep a tender eye on Gina.

I made it home and told Dan what had happened. He didn't think I was crazy, so I felt reassured, able to trust what would become clearer over time.

The next morning, as I wrote notes about that first class meeting, a Communication Studies class that focused on narrative medicine, another spiral-surge engulfed me. I had been leaning across the bed writing in my journal when it began. I turned and sat on the floor, holding the energy and the imagery, staying with it as best I could, sensing that it was transformational and thus trustworthy energy. I felt again the presences of specific friends, living and dead, as well as several students, all female. The need to wail filled me. I sat on the floor rocking and sounding—my throat blooming with immense sorrow, gusts of pure sorrow for the suffering of people throughout the world. Our gray cat came upstairs and rubbed against me as comfort.

The following day, I went to Frost Bank to retrieve something for my son Daniel, who was living and working in Prague, from our safety deposit box. As I stood in the "cave of locked treasures" signing paperwork, I felt the spiral-surge again. I stopped signing and gave all my attention to remaining upright. The bank employee noticed a change in me and asked, "Are you alright?"

I nodded, said, "I just need a moment." I sensed a softly lit, inner room filled with candles burning and young women being healed or initiated, and my leadership within a ceremony. I let the beautiful, piercing sensations ripple through me, reminding me of labor pains when delivering my children. I breathed slowly, steadied enough to complete my transaction, and returned to my car where I shook and shook.

Two more times over the course of two more days, the spiral-surges filled me. Once when I was with three female friends facilitating a poetry circle, and once at home seated at my desk. Both times I felt myself to be in New Mexico, part of a ceremonial circle of women.

At one point, I went to Dan and cried as he held me. Explained that more surges had happened, and that the power of it was awesome, overwhelming. I needed to catch my breath.

Becoming Owl-Woman

January 18, 2016

Expanding the fabric of consciousness
is like splitting slowly the constrictive skin:

one an outward sloughing off
while the other shreds and sheds from within.

Neither is painless though the pain is not cruel.
Think intense stretch of molecules loosening,

opening almost beyond bearing
giving and giving beyond recognition

as massive icicle warms, thaws, drips
then contracts again—warms, thaws:

drip becomes unrelenting
solid yielding utterly to flow

then falling away with a great *crack*!

January 20, 2016

    Last night's evening class was a river of beautiful flow. For two and a half hours I felt such a sustained focus, and deep connection with students who were engaged and digging deeply into the assigned reading. The environment felt unusually collaborative and creative. I noticed how grounded I felt, deeply at home in the material as if I was breathing it. I felt unusually articulate, weaving connections between texts that intrigued students and surprised me.
    I feel more integrated; my powers of thought and feeling, sensing and relating are blended into a changed texture of being that is more spacious. It feels as if the

spiral-surges displaced and whirled me into a new center which roots me now.

January 28, 2016

    I witnessed such a beautiful moment with a student yesterday. Re'Shea is preparing herself emotionally for the trial of her brother's murderer, which she expects will begin soon. She came to poetry writing workshop class a few minutes early to share recent writing with me. She said that after she had written the first poem, a prayer poured out of her that seeks help with feeling forgiveness and help with her intention to serve the common good. As she read her poem and prayer aloud, I noticed that she projected more confidence and strength than when I had met her two years earlier, when her brother's murder was quite fresh.

    I asked her if she wanted to walk the short distance to Assumption Chapel and read her poem and prayer aloud there.

    "I might not come back for a while. I might need to cry," she said.

    "Would you like for me to come with you after class?"

    She considered and said, "Yes, I would like that. I want to release this negativity."

    Following class, we entered the golden chapel glowing with afternoon light, and we set our backpacks down. Re'Shea bowed to the altar and dipped her fingers into the holy water, then crossed herself.

    "Where would you like to stand?" I asked her quietly.

    "Up by the cross," she replied.

    I walked alongside her toward the altar. The far curved wall behind the crucifix is painted a radiant gold and features a life-sized Mary dressed in sky-blue robes bathed in radiance as she ascends.

Re'Shea stood before a small brass cross to the left of the altar, and read her prayer in an unhurried, reverent voice. Goose bumps bloomed along my skin as she read with beseeching. When she finished, we held silence.

Then she sobbed briefly and hugged me; I held and patted her, immensely moved to have shared this moment with Re'Shea.

"I used to come to this chapel almost every morning before classes my freshman year. My brother's murder changed everything. I want to start coming here again," said Re'Shea as we collected our jackets and backpacks.

I looked up and noticed the late afternoon sun pouring in through one of the stained-glass windows, illuminating the halo around an image of Jesus.

"Re'Shea, stand here for a moment!"

She stood beside me, seeing what I saw. Her eyes glowed as she said, "Oh my!"

"I hope that feels like an affirmation, an answer to your prayer."

"I think so. I think so."

January 28, 2016

In the Classroom Next to Assumption Chapel

After all these years, here I am
standing in a room of light
with its high ceiling and windows
that look into the pecan trees outside
the golden chapel, where a woman
in blue robes ascends
within human view as if to suggest
we too can lift and be lifted,
bathed in divine breath, some

Words Make a Way Through Fire

of which is our own. After all these years,
here I am listening to the core
of deep hearts finding their voices,
words rising into outstretched palms
as students speak their poems,
like new buds just emerging
in those trees, rising into waves
of light, light that cracks open
the resilient pecans, light that swirls
Mary upward as she bids us
to follow, follow the light
breaking open at our feet.

January 29, 2016

I have completed my requirements for the practitioner of poetic medicine certification process! John will read my research essay and provide feedback. He expects to be in Austin in April, leading a weekend poetic medicine workshop. Perhaps we can create a circle to mark my completion.

Starting here, I catch the lift
of a spiral that has always
been, always been thickening
and thinning, tightening and
loosening, whirling inwardly
and outwardly,
      weaving my breath.
Starting here, I pledge myself
to mindfully serve and
witness, traveling
    the energies
        of the circle.

Becoming Owl-Woman

March 15, 2016

I am the wound
and I am the wound healing
and I am she who makes space for the wound
to heal, gives it a vision
beyond its own ragged gaping pain—
I am she who asks the wound
to open, allow the torn skin or muscle or bone
to knit itself, bridge itself whole again
while remembering ragged pain
       as a doorway
          from the wound
             into a new world.

March 22, 2016

    We are back from Spring Break, and I had an amazing conference with Gina, my tall, blonde-haired student from the narrative medicine class. She had never written poems before my class. She is eager to share them with me, especially ones that have emerged spontaneously and not in response to one of my prompts.

    As she read them aloud, I noticed that her face was no longer a mask. The muscles around her eyes and her mouth have loosened. Several times she smiled. Gina told me that she lost her father to cancer barely a year ago. She paused from her reading while her eyes filled with tears. She spoke about being beside her father when he died.

    "Poetry is so liberating," she said. "I feel able to breathe again having written these poems. I have tried grief counseling, but it didn't work for me. Counseling felt so awkward, I couldn't find my words. Poetry has given me my voice. I am dyslexic, so writing is usually such an agonizing process. Not so with poetry."

Her words continue filling me with joy. That poetry has given her more breath and her voice. That she can feel at home in written words when they flow from her heart in poems, this means the world to me.

March 28, 2016
In this morning's dream I seek the beach.

The light is low on the horizon as I enter the waves which feel like fluid shadows. The water is warmer than I expected, given that the air is cool. I swim alone near the beach in gently tumbling waves, blending into the water. Why has it taken me so long to enter the sea?

As daylight turns into shadow, the current strengthens, pushes me away from shore, farther out into the ocean. I look up from my swimming to assess what has changed. A man is beside me now. He says a river is emptying into the sea, right there before us. We feel the force of this river emptying itself into a larger body of water.

I am grateful for his company in these surprising, shifting waters. We find a way to swim the edge of the strong current, edge where the force of the river's flow into the ocean eases. We shape our swimming path around this edge toward the gentler tide. The current loosens its hold, and we know that we will make shore before darkness comes.

Chapter 14

Swimming as Means of Reconnecting the Split Self

Along with enduring practices of keeping a journal and writing poems, I have been a year-round swimmer since my mid-twenties. My body and spirit crave outstretched, sustained movement through water. I need to swim for long periods of time three or four times a week to feel internally settled and whole: emotionally and physically balanced.

I have often wondered why swimming is vital to me, why it brings me joy and equanimity. Once I found my natural swimming rhythm, I understood how soothing it is to be held by a bodily rhythm that involves my entire body—arms, legs, trunk, neck, and breath. To be immersed requires entering into the element and accepting a paradox. The paradox is that when swimming, I am both flowing through the water and resisting its currents, especially if the wind is ruffling the surface water against my forward motion. To some extent, water makes way for me, and yet it has its own momentum, depths, temperature, clarity, or obscurity.

I experience both flow with the water and my own strength distinct from the power of the water's currents. Resistance, flow, resistance, flow. My intuitive mind and my spirit are activated all the more. I listen to the moment with all my being.

Only recently have I realized that because of the wholistic nature of swimming, how it involves the entire body, engages muscles throughout the body, and requires patterned breath, my split self has become more thoroughly reconnected. I am entirely present and safely held.

I Listen by Covering My Ears with a Swim Cap

I listen by entering the water,
feel my body leave solid ground,

give up surface and swim into what
opens then closes quietly over my head,

swim through the shining, the shadows
asking my limbs, my hands to reach out

further than they think they can go,
find the rhythm that holds

all surrender, all outstretching
into one extended pouring of self,

core of my body enacting such rhythm,
feel my body as a flowing horizon,

feel how my spine holds
this swimming music

water and body a shared song,
wordless song of my humming soul

that pulses thanks, thanks
to All that bears me body and soul.

Swimming as Means of Reconnecting the Split Self

Once Dan and I moved into our hilltop home amid an inland ocean of green space and a backyard pool, I came to love swimming outdoors most of all. While I am grateful for the indoor pools of our nearby fitness center, as much as possible I swim outdoors, through autumn, mild days in winter, and early days of spring. Mind you, winters in San Antonio are not as persistently frigid as they are in more northern regions. I do not claim to be a confirmed member of any Polar Bear Club. Yet, I go to some unusual lengths to swim when I travel, and to swim outdoors if possible.

When I swam the Frio River years ago in late November, I wore a skin—a kind of lightweight wet suit. Now, I prefer to only wear a swimsuit, cap, and goggles. I like the feel of water against all my skin.

During my month-long writing residency at Istana Cabin, I persuaded the assistant manager of a motel in Carrizo Springs to allow me to swim their outdoor, unheated pool. I drove forty miles round trip several times a week to swim there during late winter, before spring took hold. Along with taking daily walks and shaping a daily haiku, these swims allowed me to spend six to ten hours a day writing deeply.

Outdoor water, even in a chlorinated pool, feels much more alive than indoor water. I can feel the difference. Outdoor water is charged with sunlight and with moonlight. It absorbs the breath of wind rippling across its surface. It reflects moonlight and the wings of owls flying overhead. It absorbs the sounds of birdsongs, coyote howls, and the calls of hawk.

Besides, when swimming outside, I can swim a while on my back and give thanks for the vastness of the blue sky overhead. When swimming freestyle and turning my head to lift just barely above the surface to breathe, I catch sight of cloud banks shifting. I am constantly reminded that I live within a natural, transcendent order that is always present and always changing through the course of a day, through the course of a season.

As my parents have aged into their nineties and struggle with depression, dementia, and fractures due to falls, I often feel wrapped in a tragic family tapestry, one that isn't finished yet because of the ongoing psychological suffering of my parents. Writing this book helps contain my deep sorrow and infuse spiritual meaning into the tapestry. Yet, still I ache. This activates my need to swim in winter water as a way of coping with grief. When I am grieving the loss of a loved one, or a rupture in an intimate relationship, or the loss of an elder's sense of belonging and joy in life, I feel compelled to swim outdoors more often. I came to understand this as I wrote the poem "The Water Ahead Is Cold."

Intense and unexpected loss shocks me. Jolts me. When I am shocked, I also experience fear, then grief. This tangle returns me to memories of feeling fractured, dislocated, especially by witnessing David's suicide. While I rarely blank into dissociation any longer, my body remembers what it was like to feel split from my feelings. The resonance has lessened considerably, yet an imprint remains.

Swimming as Means of Reconnecting the Split Self

The Water Ahead Is Cold

Blue sky dissolves above. The water ahead is cold,
dreadfully cold. Yet I bare myself
into the December pond—answer to insistence that I listen
to Body's craving for cold,

trust that this is a shock we can absorb.
Jolt of immersion
penetrates my being, my whole being—OH—our
whole being: now I see—

such deliberate disruption summons all of me:
every drifting / hidden part,
every molecule kindles to the need of Now, solidifies,
builds an inner fire

and declares: *You are all here—held* within familiar
    swimming rhythm
that glides and guides
body and mind like an arrow cleaving through astonishment,
through fierce bite,

into the bright beyond. All horizons of blue, all traces of
    warmth
hearth within—until
the sun, my Soul glows along my skin, warming the water
as I go.

Chapter 15

David's Hair and His Childhood Diary, 1963

On our father's ninetieth birthday in 2018, my brothers and I gather in Cincinnati with Dad and Janet to celebrate. Dad is in the early stages of dementia; he wants to tend to certain family matters while he still is fairly cognizant. We look through old boxes, finding high school yearbooks and diplomas. Then, wrapped in thick paper towels, we find David's fair hair, cut about a week before his suicide.

It is startling how untouched by time is his hair. How alive. It is astounding to touch something that once was part of David's physical being.

Grief pierces our father who walks away and wails, "No! No! No!" Following quite a few minutes of venting his feelings, Dad returns to the living room, and we hug him.

I feel sadness for the person that David did not have the chance to become. I miss him, and this missing feels so pure, focused, and unconfused by other feelings.

I miss the self-actualized man he could have become. I miss the meaningful work he might have discovered. I miss knowing the soulmate he might have married, and the children he might have fathered. I feel sadness that he did not live long enough to transmute his profound psychic pain into something treated and bearable. Something befriended, meaningful, and

David's Hair and His Childhood Diary, 1963

creatively expressed. I feel his loss cleanly, with sorrow and without agony, without imagery of his death. Miss his life, our shared life—the future he did not have, and a future that none of his family members could journey with him.

We all agree that when Dad's remains are cremated someday, David's hair will enter the fire with him. Their blending will be interred at Indian Hill Church. I welcome having a place to visit that holds some of my brother's remains. This feels literally like grounding.

Dad's dementia continues eroding his memory and his capacity for patience. No longer is he the man of my childhood and earlier adulthood. No longer does he feel rooted in a sense of self that is pleasurable, hopeful.

After Noel, Peter, and I return home from the weekend celebration of Dad's birthday, Dad places the box with David's hair in a location that he won't be able to recall four years later. I spend hours in November 2022 trying fruitlessly to locate the box at DeMar. About a month later, Peter discovers it outside the main house in the unheated, dusty, and termite-damaged family room that is crammed with moldy, discarded books and stored family belongings. I feel resentful of and angered by my father's placement of David's remains into this neglected space. How could Dad not have recognized that his son's hair deserved to be kept in a sacred, warm space within the home?

Dad's inability to honor David's hair is more about the tragic impact of dementia eroding judgment than my father's inherent nature. I need to recognize this and forgive my father. A poem steps forward and begins speaking. I channel the anger and sense of disconnect that I feel toward this situation into this poem. Writing the poem helps me to forgive my father's lack of sensitivity. It also allows me to articulate the great situational irony of hair outliving its person, serving now as a historical testimony to someone no longer living.

Words Make a Way Through Fire

Looking for My Brother's Hair

Nowhere can I find it: David's straight blond hair,
once shoulder-length, clipped forty-nine years ago,
wrapped in paper towels then placed in a shallow box.
As close to a suicide note as we ever found.

It is nowhere in the small space that once was his bedroom,
room that Dad cleared and made his own.
Not in the drawers with Dad's woolen sweaters.
Not in the closet with the lace-up leather shoes.

Not on the shelves atop Dad's books, arranged
and labeled by subject: reproductive rights,
information technology, the politics of health care.
Not in the cubicle where Dad never did

begin the book he planned to write.
Not on the shelf in the front closet beside the winter hats.
Not in the linen closet with bars of unscented soap.
Not in the kitchen closet amid boxes of herbal teas.

The only other place to look is the unheated, termite-ravaged
Family Room where books and an oak table decompose.
Surely, even with early-stage dementia, Dad would
not dismiss his son's hair to such a frigid place of ruin.

Better to believe my brother's hair is missing,
like David was fifty years ago, before hitchhiking
home with stories too troubled to tell.

During Dad's ninetieth birthday gathering, we also find David's childhood diary given him by Mother. David was eight years old at the time. Mother had inscribed a beautiful message

David's Hair and His Childhood Diary, 1963

inside the front cover of the diary, one that feels terribly ironic in today's light:

Dear David,
  At the end of the year I promise you a nickel for every day you have written something that will someday give your son a new idea of the kind of boy you were once upon a time.
  Much love,
  Your mother (January 1963)

David wrote daily for several weeks, and then stopped completely on January 18. I notice how enthusiastically he writes about school at first, especially the joy of learning cursive and learning about writing a letter, which he soon does—a letter to our grandmother Ta who is dying of colorectal cancer in Kansas City, Missouri. I notice how he enjoys swimming. I also notice a shift in tone that follows the battering by the boys at the Y. Perhaps I shouldn't read too much into this, but it strikes me as significant. The following is quoted directly from David's journal without any edits.

"Today my mother sewed on my coat buttons.
At school all of us had to write a long story about the New Year. We also had to begin carrying.
  Wednesday, January 2, 1963"

"Every one in my class did review work. We all had a story to do, reading books to do and carrying to do. But the thing I liked best was learning the names of a letter and they are: heading, greeting, body, closing and signature. We learned to do the *i* and *t* in cursive writing and here they are: *i t.*
  Thursday, January 3, 1963"

Words Make a Way Through Fire

"After school I went to the Young Mens Christian Association. Boy it sure is fun! What I do there is I first go to jim then I have a swimming and last of all I have free swim. Today at school I did a addition test, cursive writing and a spelling test.
 Friday, January 4, 1963"

"Today is not a school day. When we were going home in our car my mother asked me if I would like to play chess and I did. Cyra Jane Cain my cousin is going to spend the night.
 Saturday, January 5, 1963"

"Some people go to church today, but we didn't. All of the children, even me, had shows all of them were fun. Today Jeffrey Okeef (my best friend) came over and we had lots of fun. Also Dug Cain and Connie Cain (my cousins) came over. Dug was ruff.
 Sunday, January 6, 1963"

"Today Cousin Lilien is 94 years old. Also Cousin Cyrus was buried in Washington. Father is with Oma. At school all of us learned the letters *P* and *J* in cursive writing and here they are: *p j*.
 Monday, January 7, 1963"

"Oh boy, I sure had fun today! In our Cursive Writing I had to make some new words and here they are:
 moon tap map putting pudding
 We played Freese Tag.
 Wednesday, January 8, 1963"

"At the Y.M.C.A. ruff time.

David's Hair and His Childhood Diary, 1963

I got battered up by the boys.
Nothing happened at school.
      Friday, January 11, 1963"

"I went to the Y today.
At a resterrant I ate my lunch. (I bought it!)
My father came and we swam.
      Saturday, January 12, 1963"

"Tomorrow is a school day but who cares.
Today it was dull, very dull.
It rained and rained I had know fun.
      Sunday, January 13, 1963"

David's childhood diary travels home to San Antonio with me. Reading and re-reading David's childhood diary gives rise to this poem:

Words Make a Way Through Fire

Unfilled Pages

Dear David,
At the end of the year I promise you a nickel
for every day you have written something
that will someday give your son a new idea
of the kind of boy you were once upon a time.
*   Much love,*
*   Your mother (January 1963)*

There is that moment inside the morning darkness
where all things feel possible, where the imagination loosens

from gravity and history, when I find, as I stand at my kitchen
window, holding a black diary with a cracked leather spine,

that instead of sun glinting off the neighbor's dented red car
it dazzles the wide back of a swiftly-moving river. And,

instead of being his sister, I am my brother's grown son
tearing an unfilled page from his father's childhood diary

to write this poem, because once upon a distant morning
David survived well past his 19th birthday.

Chapter 16

David Speaks: An Extended Monologue

What follows is an imagined monologue of David's thinking and feeling the night that he died. This emerged many years ago, when I first began writing the earliest version of this book. It conveys what he might have felt, reflected, remembered, and experienced after he had fatally burned himself, yet before he perished.

I don't remember much about writing this monologue. I know that at times it flowed over the course of weeks. At other times, I pieced bits together as I thought about his life in terms of moments, moments I might have shared with him or heard him talk about or heard other family members or friends recall. Dad gave me a book of poems by Robert Frost that David had given him as a present. I read through the book, and stayed open to which Frost poems might speak to David's life at this point.

Before starting to shape this monologue, I considered long and hard whether it was presumptuous for me to write anything imagined as David's voice. How could I possibly know? I didn't feel that I knew David well; our embodied relationship was cut short. I asked David's spirit for guidance as to whether or not this was an appropriate use of creative expression.

Words Make a Way Through Fire

One day, I felt compelled to begin writing in my brother's voice. I thought it would be a few pages. It kept growing and expanding. David had a lot to say. Eventually, I found a few letters he had written during his travels in the Mercedes, and a letter he wrote me while I was away at summer camp.

During these first weeks, I was tucking my five-year-old daughter into bed one night when she asked me an odd question: "Did Hermes show Uncle David the way to the underworld?"

"I don't know. He might have done so."

"I feel Uncle David in the room with me sometimes," she said without trace of fear.

I had not talked about what I was writing. That my daughter sensed David's spirit nearby affirmed my sense that David was present as a creative collaborator. This comforted me greatly.

When Mother first read this monologue, she came to me with tears in her eyes. She told me that it felt real, like David's voice. This means the world to me.

David Speaks

Forgive me, my body. What have I done! Forgive me, my family. What have I done!

I wish I could tell you why I lit that match. Entered fully into fire. Became a torch. Something in me craved that blaze, its wild and ferocious energy. Once the scorch of heat rooted in my skin, I was no longer me. At least, not the me that I once knew.

I'll try speaking what I can recall before it all fades.

In those moments ago, before the fire, taking my own life made sense. I felt so fallen between the cracks of realities that the only way out was to dematerialize my physical self. My heart was a spinning spiral of darkness and light. Moods loomed through my head—clouds of unknowing, clouds of things hovering as if they were just about to appear. I could never get things quite clear, not for long.

David Speaks: An Extended Monologue

Have you ever sensed something wanting to pour out of you—an idea, a dream? I was going to build an underground house once. I could see the round rooms, smell the dirt hugging the walls, hear the muffled living below the surface noise. Where did that dream go? It was so real living inside my head. But you have to have land, digging equipment, architect plans, money.

All day long, I felt at such a distance from everything, even my own body. As I walked the fields earlier with Daddy's friend Peter surveying his land, I floated in and out of focus like fog. An image from a dream kept creeping into my vision. I was soldering some branches back on a tree when my hands became the blowtorch. The tree burst into flame and a turquoise-colored bird flew out of the top singing, "When the saints go marching in!"

My hands felt hot all day. As I tried concentrating on helping Peter, I thought my hot hands would melt my lighter and the surveying tools we used.

What is time when suddenly you are fire!

Entering that fire hurt like hell!

The sound of it! The roar and breath of an immense welding torch. The first bite was pure torture. My hair sizzled—quick kindling. Then my bones became branches. I no longer had skin. Blood burned inside my veins.

Remember that summer when Dad took us to the Tetons? That electric jolt of deep down cold every time we dove into Jenny Lake? Oh, if only Jenny Lake had been nearby!

How could I know how infinitely and indescribably painful one moment could be.

I ran toward your light, Cyra, the thin glow from your window. I wanted to throw myself into your arms, feel once again the comfort of skin on skin, have you tear the torch from me, roll it into a small ball where we could stamp it out together and return to the former current of our lives.

Words Make a Way Through Fire

Finally, that moment when I no longer felt terrible pain. The peace of numbness. I became pure swirling, orange blossom.

I had moved outside of time and was incredibly alive, swimming luminous as a comet against the falling night. I felt invincible, weightless. To be this light forever, a beacon from the dark heart of winter.

The blossoms spoke a Robert Frost poem: "Some say the world will end in fire. / Some say in ice. / From what I've tasted of desire / I hold with those who favor fire."

When I noticed you on the other side of heat, when you shouted, "Roll!" I became the wrestler again. To you, it may have seemed like a split second. For me, the roll lasted centuries. I tried gaining the upper hand with my fire, pinning the elusive muscles down, but my opponent matched me move for move. I paused and saw the great divide unveil, that seam between realities jagged and quick as a bolt of lightning. I understood that this letting go would be final.

As I stood up from my wrestling, never had I felt more alive. Beyond the need for hope and the measure of minutes.

There was something about the shine in your hair as you bolted back into our home, where we were received no matter how long we'd been away on the road. Wanting now more than anything to live, I followed you. Ducked as the flames and I went through the front door; I wasn't sure we would fit. Somehow, we squeezed through the narrow doorway of your shower. The spray of water I heard. Billows of rising smoke told me that the blossoms were extinguished.

I needed space, more space for breathing. It was dark as my legs moved down the hallway toward my bathroom. No longer the core of such roaring light. I thought I should feel cool, but my skin was past feeling.

Then you were back again, saying, "I love you." Your words drifted like bits of ash. I thought I might float in between them

David Speaks: An Extended Monologue

but then such heaviness! I could only stand and wait. I began feeling sad for you, for how this torching had scorched you. How could I expect you, or anyone, to understand?

One of the paramedics asked me my name. Some voice answered, "David." They helped me step from the bathtub, wrapped me in white bandages. I imagined myself as a giant moth slipping back into its cocoon ready to grow into something new. Inside me surged a regathering.

The siren lashing the air startled me at first, but the soft voices of the people nearby were stronger, like birds humming from invisible trees. They did things to my arms, and I had these tiny hoses running from me; I kept thinking of two small boys drinking milkshakes, making ice cream storms by blowing through their long straws.

Just a little longer, I thought. My sister, I have a sister out there somewhere, and brothers, and a mother, a father. One more time, let me see them one more time. I drifted on waves of voices around me, as if in a harbor, waiting.

The bright lights at the hospital were quiet and flat; they didn't dance or ripple. I felt lonely for my blooming. Always there were gentle voices. The hair of one nurse shone like yours did. She put her face down close to mine and looked right at me, brought me back from my drifting. Her hand upon my wrapped shoulder was almost warm.

Wrapped in white, I felt unsure whether I was human anymore. The smell of gasoline and of smoke clung tight as the bandages on me. My body felt spent, consumed. Yet something inside me flickered. The fire had moved inward! I thought sparks might ignite my eyelids. I tried seeing if I could burn through the bandages.

"What am I, what have I done?" I wanted to ask, but my tongue had swelled like a python in my mouth.

The nurse seemed to read my thoughts. "You're at the burn

unit at the hospital. We will help you." Then she was floating across the ceiling, her hair unbound and trailing like seaweed. She whispered, "Give me your pain. We will turn it into a little pot, a pot for storing acorns." I laughed.

Then I noticed that I could see perfectly, no glasses.

The darkness lapping against the hospital windows drew me. I flowed right through the glass and flickered like a breeze outside the tall brick walls. A VW van pulled into the parking lot. It was Dad. He didn't stop to lock it behind him although his briefcase and suitcase were visible on the back seat, reflecting the streetlights. Such an anguished look on his face. It startled me back to my body to wait until I could see you all again.

I understood that I would die soon.

I have often welcomed silence, found it quite alive, stirring with tiny invisible beings that become clear only when you place them beneath a lighted microscope. Tiny-celled creatures propelling themselves with long tails. Would death be like this silence, empty until you tune into the emptiness and hear the pulsing, the fullness? Would I be able to see your faces again? Would I have the capacity to remember, to desire an ongoing connection? Would there finally be a way of speaking that satisfied even myself?

What obligations will I have toward the living when I am dead? What obligation will I have toward you, Cyra, who saw me become fire?

I realized as I returned to my body, all physical feeling burned away, that there are more than five senses. The spirit is a sixth sense. It bears all kinds of feelers, receptors like the skin. It can see what is not visible, hear through silence, smell what emits no odor, taste past all longing, and touch on levels that make skin irrelevant. Without sensation, I could stand outside of time if only for those moments before I died, crisscrossing back and forth, between boundaries.

David Speaks: An Extended Monologue

Sometimes when I look at Mother, I see my whole history reflected in her wordless eyes, the days before breath even. I almost feel myself floating, my feet pushing off something springy.

I remember Ta, her kind face bending over me. And the way Mother spoke of her through the years, Ta continues to be real, alive in this very air which once passed through her lungs—this air that I can no longer smell.

I suddenly see Granpappy before me dressed in his three-piece suit, the chain of his gold pocket watch swaying slightly as he rises from the velvet couch in his living room with the heavy drapes—where the only way I could tell whether it was day or night was to look out the front door. He jabbed at the air with his cigar and said, "A self-respecting young man does not wear his hair long as a mop. He takes the time to be well-groomed and to polish his shoes. Perhaps that is why you have yet to secure employment! You look like a beatnik!"

I also see him sitting on the red leather couch in our living room flipping through plastic pages of his Roman and Greek coin collection, coins collected from antique shops in Berlin, Bombay, and New York City, and telling us stories about them—Nero, Constantine, Julius Caesar. Telling us that the olive branches symbolized peace. At least he left part of himself with us. Those coins, even the furniture, uncomfortable as it was. When we hold those coins in our hands, we recall his fingertips yellowed from cigar smoke pointing to them.

It was awful how his strokes eroded his sharp-edged mind. Remember how he would sit at our dining room table before an empty place mat and pretend to drink soup from a bowl or cut potatoes with a knife that wasn't there? That bowl was real to him, that spoon, that knife. He savored the salty warmth of that soup. Just because we could not see them doesn't mean those things didn't exist. I see the soup spoon before me now, a kind of floating offering from some place the body can't yet see.

Words Make a Way Through Fire

Oh, some other world throbs out there, some world beyond your walls. From the corners of my dim eyes, I've seen it glimmer. Felt it ripple through my room sure as cigarette smoke.

I didn't know until now how much I could trust the veins of light among the shadows. You see, before there was such noise! The clattering of my doubts—should I stay in school, or sign up for Outward Bound? Am I really crazy or just terribly confused? Who am I really? Will I know the right thing to do when it speaks to me?

What do I leave behind? For what will you remember me? What do I take with me? What shall I find?

I sense another knowing, opening up.

I am hearing something strange. At first, it seemed to ripple from the lights, but now I hear it inside my ears, as if a minuscule amplifier has been implanted. It speaks my name with such tenderness! Part of me is melting. I feel less afraid.

I see myself walking underground, carrying a single lit match that never burns down. I see only one step at a time—sense solid rock opening as I edge slowly through it. I lose all sense of body. I feel like a snake, all belly and sliding through an unknown crack between worlds, lighting my way with my glowing tongue.

My tongue smells the heat first, long before I feel the light. So odd, this heat amid the coolness. I stop and consider. A voice says, *Come closer. I mean you no harm.* I continue. I ripple forward and all the rock dissolves. The light grows, flares into a giant heart of fire that does not scorch me as I stare into the beautiful pulsing.

My face shines on a single strand of fire. I see the faces of everyone I have ever loved or who has loved me. I want to slip from my snakeskin and into the heart.

Oh, my parents, there you are—here by my bedside. Cyra.

David Speaks: An Extended Monologue

Now I begin to see the magnitude of what I leave behind. Noel, Peter. Forgive me the grief I leave you. The terrible questions.

Oh, come closer! Closer. Bend your heads down close to my mouth. Let me tell you this gateway was not your fault. So many words jumble.

Words stick to my mouth, my slow-moving tongue.

Robert Frost speaks for me: "There was never a sound beside the wood but one, / And that was my long scythe whispering to the ground. / What was it that whispered? I knew not well myself; / Perhaps it was something like the heat of the sun, / Something, perhaps, about the lack of sound— / And that was why it whispered and did not speak."

Love and regret, such twins. Don't leave now, don't leave!

After you all left my bedside, I went wandering again. Something felt faintly familiar about the hospital. At first I thought I had emerged in Seattle, that my bandages were really a straitjacket and everyone around me was in various stages of being wrapped or unwrapped. We were packages of white. Place a few red or green bows on us and deliver us as belated Christmas presents, gifts that went astray during shipping, struck out on their own to circumnavigate the world.

Then, I recalled the words of the nurse with the shining hair. "Burn unit." I thought about how in order to live I would have to grow an entire body of new skin to replace what I had damaged. How could I do that? Skin is made of millions of tiny cells. It takes six hundred thousand cells to construct a section of skin the size of a postage stamp. I need new skin, something already made, ready to slip into like a wet suit.

New skin, where can a person find new skin in a place like this? I drifted in and out of many corridors before I located the nursery. So many newborns swaddled in white blankets, small caps on their heads, only their peaceful faces growing out of the

Words Make a Way Through Fire

wrapping. One baby, a boy, had just been bathed. He was the color of a copper penny that's been carried around in people's pockets for a few years. He was either mad or hungry because he was really sounding off, hands waving, ribs pressing like tiny buttresses against his fresh skin. As the nurse dried him, I floated right alongside his face and sang, "Oh, when the saints go marching in, oh, when the saints go marching in." I swear that boy stopped crying and looked right at me with eyes dark as my boots when they were new.

Even the nurse noticed as she slipped a clean diaper on him and dressed him. She said, "Well, there now, you finally stopped your fussing."

His miraculous skin disappeared inside folds of blanket. His curly strands of hair disappeared inside a blue-and-white striped cap. The nurse paused to stroke his cheek. *Once more, stroke his cheek once more, for me.* She lifted him and carried him to his bassinet, where she placed him upon his back, stroking his quiet cheek once more before turning to the next baby.

So many children with their perfect skin. How many children would it take to have enough skin to cover me? Fifteen, twenty-three? What a patchwork I would be, a human quilt of flesh tones—all shades from white to brown to dark as a moonless night. All over me would be these small baggy places where newborn knees and elbows once poked through. What if their skins kept growing once they were attached to me, kept growing not knowing that they were no longer part of an unblemished life but seamed alongside the islands of many lives and stitched together to remake me? I'd end up slipping around inside my own skin of many skins, like walking around in the shoes of many others all at once, none of them a true fit. That would never do.

Just the same, I lingered awhile with the newborns before I remembered that not far from this place of beginnings was the

David Speaks: An Extended Monologue

preemie unit. Along a few more hallways and through some double doors.

As I entered, a nurse with a long black braid hung up the phone and called out to the others, "A helicopter is on the way with twins born at twenty-eight weeks at the scene of a car accident. Jackie, call Dr. Martin. A team will meet him in ten minutes by the landing pad."

I remembered this nurse with the black braid and bright blue eyes. She had been the assistant head nurse a few years earlier when Eric and I had evaluated the grounding of the monitors. She must have been promoted; the way she spoke, being in charge seemed so natural to her. It took me some time to get used to being around such tiny babies sequestered as they are in their incubators, hooked up to heart monitors, fluids feeding their veins; some wore tiny masks for breathing oxygen. It was hard to see where the baby stopped and the technology began—they needed one another. The babies so small, some barely longer than my hand, their wrists about as thick as my thumb.

The first day we worked in here one of the babies was slipping fast no matter what the doctors and nurses did. When we came back the next day, the incubator stood empty.

The monitors have changed since we were testing to see which ones might not be properly grounded. These give so much more information than the old ones did and they're smaller. The prototypes must have proven successful. I was so pleased with myself when I identified a faulty ground. To see how ideas inside your head could be used to protect a person, especially a person who depends utterly and, without knowing it, on other people and the environment they create—well, this made me want to know everything there was to know about electronics.

Electricity is amazing. It is such a part of us, an invisible part of us unlike blood or bones or hair. We can't see it or feel it inside

Words Make a Way Through Fire

of us: the leap across synapses, the flight like microscopic race cars of messages along the spine and throughout the brain. Each of our sense organs—eyes, ears, skin—has receptor cells which can read light, sound, or temperature and change it into electricity. Think of it! Light absorbed by the cells of the retina become electrical signals which the brain then decodes, turns into images. Sound waves pass through the canal of the ear, vibrate on the eardrum, travel through three tiny bones to the cochlea where the waves become electrical signals and course to the brain through the auditory nerve. All of this in less than a split second.

As our muscles contract, more electricity pulses through our bodies. We crackle within as we sleep, drive down a highway, change a record on the stereo. Electricity keeps us alive and moving and doing and knowing.

Is it electricity that gets us going, quickens somehow when conception occurs and the dance of the DNA begins? Does the DNA talk through electrical impulses, heat up imperceptibly as information is exchanged, intertwined and layered into billions of cells, each with a function? What fuels that first unseen spark, that unobserved bang that gets the tiny heart pumping even before all the chambers are fully formed? What finally causes the current to cease, no more sparks, leaps of contained fire? When we die, is it like being unplugged?

Like God, electricity is invisible except as lightning, and no one really knows what it is.

Even a single drop of water carries an electrical charge. Lightning begins in water droplets gathered inside a cloud. If the voltage becomes strong enough, a current begins to flow through the droplets. Sparks can arc from one cloud to another or from a cloud to the ground. From the silence of water to the sizzle of light. What a trip!

I read somewhere that amber can produce sparks when rubbed hard enough. Years ago, I bought several chunks of

David Speaks: An Extended Monologue

amber from a rock store. Made a small pyramid of sticks and started rubbing the amber above it. I rubbed and rubbed but all I felt was the heat of friction.

Soon, my body will no longer be like amber. I imagine my family will finish the job I began and cremate me, cremate my remains.

My remains. What an expression for a dead person's body. What will remain of me? My useless body, damaged beyond repair. Where will my thoughts go, my feelings, my memory? Where will the energy of all my living go? Surely, it can't be simply erased without a trace anywhere? What is the point if our lives don't inscribe permanently somewhere? What religion is it that talks about The Book of Life? Islam? Will my life, my name be recorded on the pages of some gigantic book in the library of God? Will any scrap of me remain me, David Rockwell Duff Sanborn? A small spark hovering about a campfire, making its way toward a star? A free-floating current in search of a conductor?

Will I know what I have become one way or the other?

Welding in high school was a rush for me. Using blasts of blue and orange fire to bond pieces of metal. I nicknamed my welding torch Dragonbreath. I felt almost like a god holding fire in my hands, making new shapes. What is it about fire for me? About charged light flowing through wire, on the verge of bursting into flame? To control pure seething energy. Maybe I was Vulcan in another life.

Have you ever noticed, Cyra, that there's no such thing as total darkness? What seems black at first becomes shades of gray—charcoal gray, slate gray, green-gray, blue-gray, silver. Your eyes adjust, dilate as they lock onto barely visible traces of light. Gray for me has always been a comfortable place because it's so full of color. Daylight can be too glaring. Give me the night!

Words Make a Way Through Fire

I went through a phase where I'd wake up at night and couldn't go back to sleep. I'd start obsessing. The silver shimmered and spiraled out of the corner of my eyes. The light threading through the darkness quivered, almost breathing. One night, it made me feel so crazy that I took my flashlight and went quietly into your room, just for comfort. You were lying on your left side, sleeping peacefully. I wanted so much to feel peaceful again, to feel like I did the night of the new snow long ago.

Your hair spilled across your pillow in strands like small, dark snakes. I sat by your bed for a long time, listening to you breathe slow and deep. I didn't need the flashlight. The shades of gray arranged themselves into patterns I recognized. I felt calmer, my heart stopped playing basketball inside me. You stirred. Part of your leg peeked through the covers. I watched it resolve into a small light surrounded by shadow. Without thinking, I slowly eased the covers off a larger portion of your leg as if I was unearthing more light. Then I worried that your leg might become chilled by the night air, so I shone the flashlight along your skin as if to warm it. Light upon light.

I wondered what it was like to be a girl. If I had been a girl, my life would be so different—I wouldn't worry about my draft number. I wouldn't have hitchhiked all across the country either or been safe in some of the places where I've stayed. As I thought about how vulnerable you were, the circle of light on your leg began fading. I needed more light, so I pulled the sheet off a little more.

Your voice startled me although it was soft enough. When you asked me what I was doing, I couldn't remember what had brought me there. I felt utterly strange, outside myself. When I told you I was crazy it was as if someone else was using my voice for his words. I think you knew it too because you didn't buy it.

David Speaks: An Extended Monologue

I felt so depressed when I returned to my room. The flashlight could hardly hold its light. I lit a cigarette and blew smoke rings. Thinking *maybe if I concentrate hard enough I can make rainbow-colored smoke rings like Gandalf, the wizard in The Hobbit*. Surely there is some power in me. Some power beyond the electrical.

Even wizards have their limitations. When the dwarves and Bilbo were trapped in the tall trees of Mirkwood Forest, wolves snapping at their heels and goblins fast approaching with mad glints in their eyes, what could Gandalf do to save himself and the others? Conjure fire and cast it down among the wolves. Some wolves caught afire and ran howling. Not being made of fur, the goblins weren't afraid. They spread the fire cast down by Gandalf to the trees sheltering Bilbo and the dwarves. They all would have died if the eagles hadn't plucked them from the blazing trees just in time. What a story! The making of a hero out a fat furry hobbit, a creature of tunnels and comfort.

I really did believe I would build a hobbit house someday. I drove to that house in Indian Hill that was built like a horseshoe into a hill. Remember that one? All you could see from the driveway was the glass entranceway. From the front door the arms of the house disappeared left and right into low hills, almost like long burial mounds. I had the nerve to climb out of the Mercedes and ring the doorbell. I half expected Bilbo to answer in his bobbing way. But nobody was home. Through the glass, I glimpsed a hint of fluid green and realized that the house wrapped around a pond on the other side.

The comfort of being underground, submerged and sheltered. How quiet such a house would be with the good earth piled snugly all about it. I would want long hallways leading like tunnels far into the round mound of the hill. A few rooms would need windows so that I could keep an eye on the waxing of the moon, and just in case it snowed during the dark hours.

Words Make a Way Through Fire

What would I keep in my pantries? Bilbo dearly loved food. I want a giant freezer full of Mom's sticky buns. I'd need a library, two libraries really—one for books and one for records. I would wire a stereo system where every room and hallway had sound. Plug in the toaster and out blares Jimi Hendrix along with crisp cinnamon toast! There would be a room with only a ping-pong table inside of it that glowed in the dark. A welding room! I'd have a studio just for welding—sparks flying all around me as I worked the metal hidden under the hill.

"Be it life or death, we crave only reality." Thoreau was so right.

I can't decide if reality is all out there in the needles of the pine trees, in the density of the ground, or if it's as insubstantial as our thoughts. Is the world real because we perceive it, or because it simply is? That answer should be easy. The planet spun in this tiny corner of the cosmos billions of years before man existed. So, then the physical world is reality—independent of our thoughts, our presence, complete with its own self-contained rules like the speed of light and the pull of gravity.

What lives in our heads permeates our pores, lives throughout our bodies. Where does the mind stop and the body begin? Where does the body stop and external reality begin? Here at my fingertips? Or just the other side of my skin in a molecule of air, a molecule of air that I may have already breathed in and exhaled, leaving the scent of my lungs on it?

I remember standing in the middle of the Colosseum in Rome, surrounded by its great curved shape and stone walls of various crumbling heights, knowing that thousands of people had been slaughtered right where I stood. I could almost hear their screams, the crunching of bone, the howling of crowds. This reality was all too alive once upon a time. Yet, as I looked, really looked at the present moment, what struck me most were the cats, thousands of cats draped on the ancient white stone. Black cats, orange tabby cats, gray cats, kittens with white paws, cats without tails spilling across steps, mating, stretching before giving themselves a bath. Not a place for a lost mouse. From glory and gore to ruins and rabies.

I also remember thinking what a great place for a Frisbee game, there in the Colosseum. I'd almost brought a Frisbee along on that trip. We could have covered some ground there in the open where the gladiators and the Christians once collected. Send that disc sailing from one end to the other. Hardly even a breeze to send the Frisbee off course.

Then I thought of Apollo 11 and the lunar module that we had watched land on the moon with just seconds of fuel to spare. To step on the surface of the moon, to step on solid ground that is not of the Earth, literally another world beyond human experience. I decided then to experience something so far beyond the ordinary that I would be forever changed.

I stood there in the Colosseum trying to imagine my future. For the first time, I felt grateful for my faulty vision, otherwise I could be faced with fighting in Vietnam within a few years. Nam, now there's a forge for turning boys into men! Burning villages, trying to stay alive in a jungle threaded with booby traps. Man, oh, man, me with a submachine gun? I'd have to hoof it to Canada. We can put a man on the moon, but we can't end a war.

I thought about how one monk helped another, poured the gasoline over his shoulders, the hands upturned on his knees, the feet, his bald head. Then probably a prayer before the match. Not a single sound from the monk within as the flames burned his robe, his earlobes, his eyebrows. A shower of flame. Does such an action change anything? Will that help bring about an end to the war? Could I be so brave? Could I help someone else be so brave? As brave as those early Christians facing the lions.

There are those of us who remember. There is power in remembering. I vowed to remember those monks the rest of my life and to remember the image of a boot print on the moon.

Words Make a Way Through Fire

A boot print on a cold moon. My own fire must be thinning. I feel cold, like being licked by a single flame. What else can I claim before I go?

I remember nearly being flattened by a semi outside of Wichita! February, that cold month weighed down by ice and snow. That wild trip to California with Geof a few years back. The Mercedes was still trucking, though losing her tread. That morning we left Kansas City it started hailing and there was a patch of ice stretching from Kansas City to Wichita, especially on the highway. The annoying play in the steering wheel, which we'd discovered after leaving Cincinnati, got progressively worse as the miles went by. Plus, the heater wouldn't work. Geof lost the car once on a snowy curve and got kind of sideways. Later, I was driving and got blown off the road by a semi. We went into a ditch dividing the two opposite lanes, took down two reflectors and ended up facing another semi coming the other way. I drove back into the ditch, then onto the westbound highway. The Mercedes did all this without groaning, and without any damage to the suspension, although the front end got knocked about. Some car. Scared the wits out of the hitchhiker we'd picked up shortly after passing through Indianapolis. He seemed relieved to go on without us.

We shacked up for nearly a week in Wichita waiting for Scholfield Brothers Pontiac and Mercedes Sales and Service to receive parts for a ten-year old Mercedes. When the man put the car up on the rack, he said it had the worst front end that he had ever seen. We had more adventures trying to find a place to stay all that time. We got run out of His Place. We called it the Jesus Freak House. A paranoid schizophrenic wanted to club us with a baseball bat. I don't think he much liked our hippie hair. That and the fact that Geof would turn up the fuel on his cigarette lighter, flash a thick flame and cry, "I'm on fire for Jesus. Let me be the light."

David Speaks: An Extended Monologue

Later, we got run out of someone else's apartment by two guys who were gay and had been picked up by the roommate while barhopping. They flat out didn't like our looks. One of them tried picking a fight with me, but I refused to bite. Took my Pall Malls and went for a walk in the dirty snow. We ended up at The Bridge—a drug-oriented crisis center—until the car was ready. Watched some cat strung out on acid flip out, throwing chairs and trying to jump through a window. The counselor was ready for him, though—watching him carefully, anticipating his next move. I was watching him watch the guy. Together, we restrained him for a while. Then we helped him into a small, darkened room and put on some calming music, sounds of waves at the beach. Someone called his sister. She showed up, rubbed his back and talked real soft. Gradually, he calmed down.

We didn't quite fit in anywhere. It was such a relief to set out for Berkeley. By then, the weather had calmed down too, clear and cold. On our way back to Ohio, we took a day to bop around Kansas City. We had four dollars between us and a BankAmericard, which isn't much good short of Holiday Inn. The nicest guy at the Bluebird Motel gave us steak and baked potatoes with all the insides mashed up and free beds for the night.

All in all, I am glad that we took that cross-country trip, and were able to help out quite a few hitchhikers, but next time it will be a lot easier just to hitchhike myself! Next time? No more next times.

Let me remember spiders in the Everglades, barracudas in the coral reef. Florida. Sunburned hot. Never had I seen such big spiders clinging to giant webs strung between swamp trees. I felt like running along the trail that day. I rounded a bend and came within inches of swallowing a black spider the size of my palm. Luckily I stopped dead in my tracks. That spider didn't flick a leg as it swayed ever so slightly on a web that spanned the trail, about eight feet across.

Words Make a Way Through Fire

I had to duck under it, hoping that it wouldn't drop on me. I walked the rest of the way, ducking here and there wondering how many horseflies do spiders that size have to eat daily just to stay alive.

"Hi-de-hi. Hi-de-ho." A voice, I hear a voice. Whose voice brings me back above ground to the bright lights? The nurse with the shining hair. What is she trying to tell me? I can see her words filling up the air like bubbles. God, it's deeply cold inside my body. My underground house, that's what my body has become, under all these bandages.

The words of the nurse are popping one by one. One bubble, let me catch just one. This one, the "I am" bubble. I want to reach. My hand feels like wet sand. Reach with my mind. Cup it with the light of thought. There. It glows before me, hovering, spins ever so slowly to show me another side. Words inscribed: Time is but the stream I go a-fishing in. I drink at it; but while I drink, I see the sandy bottom and detect how shallow it is. Its thin current slides away, but eternity remains. I would drink deeper; I would fish in the sky, whose bottom is pebbly with stars.

Hard to breathe, body shutting down, fuse by fuse, no replacements. My current trickles. My current will not be current much longer. Let me fly with the fish in the sky before I die. Let me walk along the shore of the Atlantic once more. Hear the low roar of the waves breaking in their sweep toward land, their falling backward to wave again and again, a constant tumble.

Close my eyes. My God the wind has caught me, swirls me away through the dark. Everything falls away. I am lifted, should feel cold at these heights. The clouds are parting. One more look at the moon? Somewhere below a young man looks out his window at the pure silent snow. Breathe deep, my friend,

David Speaks: An Extended Monologue

breathe deep. An old man looks out too from the same window. The old man I might have become.

A fish leaps from the water and hangs motionless in the sky. We are plunging. We? Why did I say we? The fish is gone. Me, myself, and I. There's a trinity for you. To have a self and to know you have a self, even if it's unclear what such having really means.

I hear a poem forming in my mind. I wish I could write it down. I must recite it.

> Go then, put aside the basket of noise,
> sharp voices rubbing together like stones
> like false prophets.
> Stand in a quiet room, lit by one tall candle.
> Listen until time falls away, a lost bone.
> As you slowly absorb the flame,
> you'll find yourself glowing.
> You are a lantern now, full of light and resolve.
> Push through the looming shadows,
> enter the bright atmosphere of truth.

I feel the sand beneath my feet, faintly warm as if just touched by sunlight. The glistening ocean ripples, swells in all its cold and ancient tides. Between my toes something slimy. What's this—seaweed, the kind you can pop, pop, pop. Would it sting this time if I stepped on a jellyfish? Let me stand here alone, sea-foam washing over my feet, ready to be made new again.

If I listen carefully enough, perhaps I'll hear the sound of Dad's voice telling us stories back over that hill near the trees. He and Mother will know to scatter my ashes here. Be here.

Words Make a Way Through Fire

Golden Octopus: Reconnection
(With thanks to James Bridle & his *Ways of Being*)

Once upon a time, an octopus lived inside me,
clutching my heart and lungs. Golden tentacles

nestled along my rib cage and into the small of my back.
It entered when my body rushed my spirit through

the winter-dark calling calling for help.
For ten years I could scarcely breathe.

Now I know the octopus meant no harm.
It filled many cracks, strengthened my divide.

"The octopus does intelligence with its whole body,"
I read. "Its many brains extend throughout its limbs,

each arm moving and responding alone."
To be multiple and yet whole.

To explore and yet be at home:
one arm touching the rhythmic beat of the heart,

another stretching toward the stars. Slowly,
slowly my octopus unwound tentacle after tentacle,

slipped through my side and back to the sea,
leaving an emptiness I could occupy.

Left me breathing on my own
and calmed by ocean waves.

David Speaks: An Extended Monologue

Why do I dream of you now—golden octopus? Your arms
glow and flow beside me, unfurling in wordless rhythm.

Do you remember our early story? Are you calling me?
Is it my turn to dwell within you, each arm a changing story?

Is it time to inhabit many stories:
be under and over, into and alongside, here

and beyond, spiraling through
human time and ocean time

all at once?

Afterword

July 3, 2024

My Dear Brother David,

You must know—surely you already know!—that Mother died a few weeks ago. She struggled for several days to breathe, requiring oxygen, and her heartbeat was erratic. Yet, her final hours were more peaceful, Peter says. Noel played the guitar and sang for her over the phone. I told her that I loved her over the phone—it all happened so fast, her cascade toward death, within just a handful of days. The palliative care coordinator came into Mother's room twice, and sang for her. Back in October, when Mother was still in the hospital following the repair of her other broken hip, she asked me, "Why can't I move on while listening to Yo-Yo Ma?" Wouldn't that have been wonderful to have had Yo-Yo Ma playing his cello so blissfully in her room as she took her final breaths! Mother loved music so much; it could touch her soul.

I am comforted to know that she was surrounded by loving presences in the room that had become her home over the past eight months: Peter held her right hand and cousin Tia held her left hand during her final hours. By contrast, I am so so sorry that you died alone in hospital. That was a different time—50 years ago!—and we were all terribly shocked. Not thinking quite straight. Though I forgive us our oversight, our not-knowing, I still regret that you died without people who loved you by your side.

Noel and I arrived in Boston the day following Mother's death. We gathered around her remains for about 15 minutes before her body was conveyed into a portal of fire. Then, I stood outside the inner room and held my hand upon the tall wooden door as the crematorium doors rumbled open and her body entered the flames. I did all I could to accompany her spiritually as she entered that fire. For quite some time, ripples of energy flowed through my head, through my spine to my bare feet. I felt with her, David, I felt connected to Mother spiritually as her body was released into becoming bits of bone and dust. And, perhaps—I pray that it be true—you received her on the other side of fire.

After Mother's cremation, we found a beautiful chapel for her Celebration of Life. It is scheduled for the weekend before your 50th birthday. I invite your spirit to come close during the morning ceremony. We need you.

All three of us have spoken of you many times during these days. We shared stories with one another about childhood memories not spoken before. We missed you. Your living presence has been invoked.

I am home now. Getting used to my new self, without a mother. Dad is not happy about his life, living so long with dementia. You probably know that. I think he may cross over before many more months pass.

What I most want to tell you, David, is that a few minutes ago, I felt an immense longing to hug you, to enfold you into my arms in the way I could enfold Noel and Peter. I yearned to offer you comfort, and be comforted by you. I want to say between my tears how much I love you. How glad I am to have had you as my brother. How I have missed you over these years. How would our relationship have grown? What would your

Afterword

children have looked like? You would be so proud of our brothers, in their devoted care of our parents in their final, distressing years. My expanding love for them includes an ever-growing love for you too.

I understand more fully now what it was like for you growing up in our family. The specifics of your suffering as well as of your nurturing. I have heard stories previously unspoken that involved you. I now recognize so much more about the hurts carried unspoken in your heart. Perhaps more of you is apparent to me, felt by me, loved by me.

So, I hold the photo, our photo, to my chest, press it against my heart, and rock you, rock us both, imagining that you, in all your muscular kindness, live here now in my arms.

Cyra

December 30, 2024

My Dear Brother David,

Surely you must know that Dad died on December 23 a few hours before my plane landed in Cincinnati. Janet was with Dad, holding both of his hands and talking to him. She said he passed so peacefully that she didn't notice exactly when he stopped breathing. I lingered with his body before the funeral home collected him, thanking Dad on behalf of all his children for being our father. Significant family commitments kept Noel and Peter from being able to come.

Like Mother, Dad's final illness and cascade toward death happened quickly, over the course of five days. Dad had been profoundly unhappy and depressed throughout the year. When his mind was clear, he understood why his move to assisted living had been necessary; Janet no longer could care for him at home safely. Yet, often his mind was agitated and his thoughts fixated from the increasing dementia. In those moments, Dad mourned the loss of his remarkable intellect and the loss of his shared life with Janet at DeMar. His desperation often became rage. Other times, he took to his bed and hoped to die.

Refusing to take medication consistently to soften his moods, Dad became convinced that he was responsible for your suicide. If only he had offered you a loan to buy a reliable car so you could continue working, if only he had expressed more understanding and compassion, if only he had helped you find practical solutions for your struggles, if only . . . He blamed himself no matter how we tried to persuade and reassure him otherwise.

Anger flared in me again for how your suicide inflicted decades of suffering upon our family, especially upon our parents. Then I recentered myself, and loved you again without blame, without judgment, and with a cleansing wave of pure sorrow.

Do you still remember the head of hair you left behind? A few days before your suicide, you had your shoulder-length, red-blond hair cut short, remember? Was that haircut preparation for your deadly action to come, a signal of turning point? You brought your bundle of hair home wrapped in paper towels. Dad found it weeks later in your bedroom.

Earlier today, I unwrapped your remains from the paper towels. I marveled at how much hair you had left behind—thick, soft, unaged—then I held the tangled mass against my heart and lifted it toward the bright December sky as petition for blessing. Next I rewrapped your hair in a clean linen handkerchief inscribed with Granpappy's monogram: FRS. Janet had just found the handkerchief inside a pocket of Dad's favorite jacket. This felt so right. The handkerchief I placed inside a small, black box—the kind of fancy box that contains something precious. Cherished. The inside was cushioned, the outside velvety and plush to touch.

I carried that box to the crematorium the way the Magi must have carried their gifts centuries ago to the luminous baby born in the manger.

Afterword

Alone inside the visitation room, I placed the handkerchief upon Dad's chest, above his silent heart. It felt like orchestrating a reunion! It felt like restoration of a deep, loving bond. A few minutes later, I pressed the button that conveyed the cardboard coffin holding Dad's body and your hair toward the flaming threshold. Entrance to the sacred fire opened.

I witnessed your return to fire, David, but this time it was fire of sacred transformation. This time you were not alone. This time I witnessed with awe and gratitude.

Peace fills my spirit—peace that follows when a terrible, prolonged disquiet has been gentled. Connection and love now have the final word.

Cyra

Words Make a Way Through Fire

Listening for Owl

I can't explain what happened or why,
don't know what it signifies or whether
it changes anything or not. I only know

that I had been missing the great-horned owl
hunting our neighborhood. It had been months
since his rhythmic call had rippled through

the dark, pierced my sleep and winged me
to the realm between flesh and shadow, where
reunions between the breathing and the buried

take place inside of dreams. I only know that
my brother long-dead filled me with his being.
The shoreline of his gaze wove seaweed strands

and infinite tides around me. His hand lightly
brushed my back as if to prove his presence;
my skin still quivers at this surprising touch.

All these years, and still we recognize each other.
Memory pulses across thresholds, in the knowing
song of owl vanishing now in this dawn while

the space inside me
that held my brother's form
is still warm.

References

Fox, John. *Poetic Medicine, The Healing Art of Poem-Making.* New York: Jeremy P. Tarcher, 1997.

Frost, Robert. Page 206: Lines quoted are from "Fire and Ice." Page 211: Lines quoted are from "Mowing."

Levertov, Denise. *The Collected Poems of Denise Levertov.* New York: New Directions Books, 2013.

Moyers, Bill. *The Language of Life, A Festival of Poets.* New York: Doubleday, 1995.

Nachmanovitch, Stephen. *Free Play, Improvisation in Life and Art.* New York: Jeremy P. Tarcher, 1990.

Orr, Gregory. *Poetry as Survival.* Athens: University of Georgia Press, 2002.

Perrine, Laurence. *Sound and Sense, An Introduction to Poetry.* 7th Edition. San Diego: Harcourt Brace Jovanovich, 1987.

Rilke's Book of Hours. Translated by Barrows, Anita and Macy, Joanna. New York: Riverhead Books, 1996, 2005

Sanford, John A. *The Kingdom Within.* San Francisco: HarperCollins, 1987.

Taylor, Barbara Brown. *When God is Silent.* Cambridge: Cowley Publications, 1998

Acknowledgments

Writing this book has been a journey of twenty-seven years. Many individuals have contributed to its content and final form over the course of its evolution. It feels almost inevitable that I will not remember each person whose generous reflection, listening ear, supportive heart, or feedback on drafts helped this story to clarify or deepen. I will do my best to recall.

Being a human being on this planet is a mysterious, marvelous, and complicated experience. Something larger holds all of this: this planet, this life, this story. It resists definition and resists any particular name. I call it Voice. Thank you for all your creative, loving, healing ways. Thank you for letting me know that you are present, aware, reaching out, empowering.

More than anyone, Dan, my husband of forty-five years, has seen me through this prolonged process of recollection and reflection with all its resonating fields of trauma, and phases of recovery. I cannot adequately express my gratitude for your enduring support. You are nurturing, holding space for me with your steadfastness, depth of character, deep love and loyalty, and sense of humor. How many freshly baked, still-warm-from-the-oven chocolate chip cookies or slices of homemade cinnamon bread have you brought me while I was writing? As I reflect now, from this perspective of having finally settled the story in this form, I realize that it wasn't until I married you that I felt secure enough to begin feeling all my shattered bits of self and inviting them back to the long, lit table. Thank you. I don't know who I would be now if not for you in my life.

I thank my children, Cyra Alexandra and Daniel Amadeus, for your love and support. Since childhood, you lived alongside the me who was writing and setting aside and returning to this book. While we didn't discuss it much, this story I was writing—my persistent need to grasp the deepest version of it and then bring it into words—was part of the common air that we breathed together—mostly implicitly, yet also explicitly. I wish I could have been a more integrated mother for you from the days you were born. Forgive my blind spots and threads of numbness. I am so proud of each of you! The meaning you give my life is immeasurable.

I embrace my first family. I thank my parents, the late Cyra Duff Sanborn and late Fred Sanborn, for your time reading earlier drafts and clarifying details. I know that my need to persist with this telling was not painless for you; you remained steadfast in your support. I am especially grateful for the stunning tree of life rug that Mother wove the winter following David's death. And I am especially grateful for the exquisite childhood photograph taken by Dad that graces the cover of this book. Thank you as well for the gift of all three of my beloved brothers.

I thank my living brothers Noel Sanborn and Peter Sanborn for your ongoing love and support. While we live in different regions of this country, we share a connection and loyalty that transcends boundaries, a bond forged in large part by the shared, terrible loss of our eldest brother. You have become such beautiful, generous, gracious, admirable men, and I am honored to call you my brothers.

David, I feel your spirit with me each day. Thank you for going to the beach with me in my healing dreams. Thank you for guiding me through the writing of your monologue; I pray that I listened carefully and deeply enough to do you some

Acknowledgments

justice. I wish I could have been a more grounded, listening, and courageous sister for you while you were living. Forgive me my youthful self-centeredness and fearfulness.

Childhood friends saw me through the earliest days of the aftermath of David's suicide. Marie Kittredge, thank you for serving as acolyte during David's memorial, and thank you for the comfort of your presence those first nights. I really feared the dark, and you softened the shadows by keeping me company. Connie Condit Derry, thank you for the hospitality of your family the day after, and for asking me to race you down the street when I was about to dissolve. Catherine Bourne Sherman, thank you for speaking your heart to me the day after, and solidifying our friendship. Thank you for taking me to the Florida Keys with your parents so I could feel something other than shock and fear. Alice Berman, thank you for offering sanctuary as my next-door neighbor, and thank you for coming outside to find and comfort me amid English Literature class when the finality of David's death hit me. Alicia Bridgeland, thank you for your empathic reads of several versions of this story.

Carol Richter Flume and the late Clay Richter, thank you for enfolding us in your warmest embrace when we came back the next morning from Richmond, Indiana, with Noel. Charles Crawley, thank you for your compassion, family friendship, and for driving.

I thank my dear writer-friends who generously and carefully responded to drafts: Melissa Shepherd, Donna Peacock, Diane Gonzales Bertrand, and Michele Stanush. Your insights made all the difference! To beloved Crones and beloved members of Poetry & Company, thank you for your many years of sustenance, friendship, incredible creativity, and courage to live with such open hearts.

Special thanks to the late Wendy Barker and Steve Kellman who championed this project in a most unexpected, transformative manner.

Words Make a Way Through Fire

Jenn Hager served as the deepest editorial responder. Your brilliant and detailed feedback allowed this book to clarify and cohere, find its final footing. I thank you for your incredibly helpful, profound, and loving critique, that often felt like healing witness.

Terri Goslin-Jones, thank you for your deep read of a nearly finalized draft. Your detailed, layered responses and insight were healing as well as useful. They also inspired me to understand the value of adding a foreword, then later an afterword.

Thank you to the late Andrea Ptak for her incredible talent, collaborative spirit, and cherished friendship. She held belief in this book for many years and steered me to Jenn Hager.

I am grateful to Dan Roloff, formerly of the H.E.Butt Foundation, for his supportive attention to and encouragement of a very early draft of this book.

Thank you to my remarkable publisher Brooke Warner and her diligent and professional staff at She Writes Press. Thank you for giving this book a publishing home.

Deep thanks to the late Alston Beinhorn for the transformative gift of the San Ysidro Ranch Writing Residency during March of 2020. The timing and affirmation of this writing residency was pure blessing. Devoting an entire month to the refocus of this book made it possible for me to complete this long-evolving story. In this context, I also wish to thank Juan Becerra who looked after me from a respectful distance during my stay on the ranch. You deftly liberated my writing space from a wolf spider that I was certain would land on me in a most ferocious manner, and you gave me a beautiful poem the day I left for home.

Clayton Milam, it is wonderful to have you woven into our family. When I look out the high window of my writing room, I see the rock garden you cultivate as well as the rain catchment systems that you have engineered and installed. All green and

Acknowledgments

blooming things seem possible then, even amid drought. My heart and soul need the nourishment of beauty that you have brought to Paradise Hill in countless ways. Thank you!

Last yet not least, the presence of soft, four-legged ones throughout the years has offered immeasurable comfort, delight, and companionship. Loving thanks to Sam, Lolita, Earl, Jesse, Buddy, Bella, Mickey, Beowulf, and Mia!

About the Author

Cyra Sweet Dumitru is a published poet and instructor of poetry, and one of four certified practitioners of poetic medicine in Texas. Her poetry has been published in numerous national literary journals as well as in many anthologies and regional publications. Her poems have also appeared in publications designed for physicians, traveled on city buses, been painted on the walls of City Hall, been sung in concerts as Art Songs, spoken on the local affiliate of National Public Radio, and spoken in dozens of museums and bookstores around the nation. Her collections of poems include *What the Body Knows*, *Listening to Light*, *Remains*, and *Elder Moon*. She offers therapeutic writing circles for adults learning to live with trauma, bereavement, depression, anxiety, and religious trauma. Cyra lives in San Antonio, Texas with her family.

cyrasweetdumitru.com

Looking for your next great read?

We can help!

Visit www.shewritespress.com/next-read
or scan the QR code below for a list
of our recommended titles.

She Writes Press is an award-winning
independent publishing company founded to
serve women writers everywhere.